The Vietnamese Australians:
Heritage and Contributions

By Minh Hiền

is released on the International Men's Day, 19 November 2023,
to celebrate
our contributions to Australian society through education and sport.

Minh Hiền with her three brothers, Sài Gòn, 1969.

The Vietnamese Australians: Heritage and Contributions narrates the contributions to Australia, spanning five decades, through education and sport by Minh Hiền and her three brothers, Trí Tri (Tri Tri Tran), Trí Tuệ (Tri Tue Tran) and Minh Trí (Tri Minh Tran). It demonstrates the positive influences of the Vietnamese culture and philosophy on people in Australia and Việt Nam. It includes a brief history of Vietnamese Martial Arts and its impacts on people, illustrated with colourful photos. Readers are also entertained with poems and proverbs. This is the second book of The Vietnamese Australians series.

For
my husband, my brothers, my father
and
those who want to know about
the Vietnamese Australians

Published in 2023 by Minh Hien Pty Limited
ABN 86 086 458 817
www.minh-hien.com

Text copyright (except texts that are acknowledged or quotes that are in the public domain) © Hien Minh Thi Tran (Minh Hiền) 2023.

Photograph copyright (except photos that are acknowledged or in the public domain or under a Creative Commons License) © Tri Tri Tran, Tri Tue Tran, Tri Minh Tran and Farshid Anvari 2023.

Cover design and book design © Minh Hien Pty Limited 2023.

Painting copyright © Ellyse Tran, Tri Tri Tran and Hien Minh Thi Tran 2023.

The moral rights of the author and the creators have been asserted.

This book is copyright.

Apart from any fair trading for the purpose of private study, research, criticism or review, as permitted under the Copyright Act, no part may be reproduced by any process without the prior written permission of the author, the photographers, the creators and the publisher.

Inquiries should be addressed to
Minh Hien Pty Limited
PO Box 737
Drummoyne NSW 1470
Australia.

This book is released on the *International Men's Day*, 19 November 2023, under the brand name *Wealthy Me* ® from the Hobart office of Minh Hien Pty Limited in Albion Heights Drive, Kingston, 7050, Tasmania.

Title: *The Vietnamese Australians: Heritage and Contributions*
Author: Hien Minh Thi Tran (Minh Hiền)
ISBN: 978-0-6459782-0-9 (Hardback)

A catalogue record for this book is available from the National Library of Australia

Minh Hiền

*Our heritage is in our hearts
and in the stories told us
by our father and forefathers.*

*Fill your head with literature
and your heart with kindness.*

*Those are treasures
you can pass on to your children.*

Minh Hiền's grandfather spoke to her father, My Heritage (p. 96)

From left to right: Minh Hiền's husband Farshid Anvari, Tri Tri Tran, Tri Minh Tran and wife Tuân Pham, Tri Tri Tran's daughter Ellyse Tran, Tri Minh Tran's daughter Emily Tran, Tri Tue Tran and Minh Hiền at the My Heritage Book Read, Sydney, 2019.

CONTENTS

Foreword	vii
Introduction	ix
Book cover photos	x
Chùa Một Cột - The One Pillar Temple	x
About the Author	xi
Our Heritage	1
Vietnamese Martial Arts	2
Saint Trần Hưng Đạo	3
Quang Trung Nguyễn Huệ	6
Bùi Thị Xuân	8
The Vietnamese Education System	10
Our Stories of Coming to Australia	17
Our Contributions	24
Education	24
The Spirit of Vietnamese Martial Arts	54
The Philosophy of Vietnamese Martial Arts	65
Optimism	69
Resilience	76
Tournaments	85
My Writing Journey	105
References	114
Acknowledgements	114

Foreword

In 1981 I was Teacher-in-Charge of the English Language Program at Mt. St. Canice Migrant Hostel in Sandy Bay, Tasmania. Amongst my students was a shy Vietnamese girl named Minh Hiền who was living with family away from the hostel. It was clear to me then, and I said as much when I wrote a reference for her at the end of the ten-week course, that she was a dedicated student with great potential. What I did not know was that many years later we would be reunited and she would allow me the privilege of writing the foreword for this book.

It is the second in the series highlighting the contribution of Vietnamese Australians to their adopted country. This particular book is an account of the role Minh Hiền and her three brothers have played in enriching Australian society through the love of learning and sharing knowledge through their dedication to the philosophy and practice of Vietnamese martial arts. Coincidentally, I also taught Minh Hiền's brother Trí Tuệ before I taught her. He too was a delight to teach. I worked with her older brother Trí Tri who was employed by the Immigration Department. I could not fail to be aware of the huge impression the brothers had on the young people who benefitted from being trained in Vietnamese martial arts. One of them Florian Sonner was the son of a German migrant whom I taught. I was invited by Florian's father to go to see his son competing in an event at the university. Minh Trí was, for me, the younger brother, still a schoolboy at that time and it is only on reading Minh Hiền's book that I have become familiar with his role in promoting and teaching Vietnamese martial arts. The family moved to Sydney and I would occasionally get news of them, but to my delight, we were reunited with the publication of her first book, *My Heritage: Vietnam fatherland motherland*.

Minh Hiền has not had an easy life. She has endured many setbacks in Australia. All of this on top of having experienced the upheaval of war in Vietnam, leaving her homeland in dramatic and dangerous circumstances and being separated from her much-loved parents. But that separation and her mother's tragic death from motor neurone disease (MND), has made her very determined to honour her mother's memory and to credit her mother with instilling the virtues of *Benevolence, Propriety, Righteousness, Wisdom and Trustworthiness* in her brothers. These virtues are evident in their wonderful contribution to Australian society. Minh Hiền has shown great generosity of spirit by creating scholarships at the University of Tasmania and the determination to assist those with whom she worked. Always looking for ways to help others, with her husband Farshid, she has developed an impressive on-line teaching program for young people in Vietnam. It has provided opportunities otherwise unavailable to them and has built links between Australia and Vietnam which have opened up horizons and potential for further study. As for me, I enjoy a delightful friendship with a shared interest in learning and writing. Australia is the beneficiary of the talents, skills and lived experience of Minh Hiền and her brothers Trí Tri, Trí Tuệ and Minh Trí.

Margaret Eldridge AM
Sandy Bay, Tasmania, November 2023.

Minh Hiền at her former high school, 1993.

Trí Tuệ, Hội An, 2023.

Trí Tri, Hobart, 1983.

Minh Trí (Bé), Hobart, late 1980s.

The Vietnamese Australians: Heritage and Contributions by Minh Hiền   p.viii

Introduction

At the core of the book lies a heart-warming story of four siblings who arrived in Australia as refugees (boat people) and held together to achieve not just for themselves but ensured to contribute to the nation that welcomed them.

Minh Hiền was a seventeen-year old refugee, in search of education, sat sail in a leaky boat. Upon arrival she enrolled in a college and soon was on her way to achieve an honours degree and continue to do a Masters in Engineering. That was not enough. Later she completed a Master of Commerce, a Master of Arts in Creative Writing, two Masters in Education and three other postgraduate qualifications. Apart from working full time, she spent a fair bit of her personal time to better the learning of her colleagues. She reached out to teach poor students in a remote part of her motherland who normally were ignored or side tracked.

The eldest-brother, Trí Tri, and the youngest brother, Minh Trí, introduced Vietnamese Martial Arts as a way of life to better the life of many who wished to improve their meditative and physical skills. They ensured Vietnamese Martial Arts is well recognised by winning championships in open competitions at National levels.

The second-elder brother, Trí Tuệ, after devoting time to Vietnamese Martial Arts, spent a great amount of time in organising tournaments for highly successful leaders of business communities in both Australia and in his motherland, many of them immigrants or refugees, to cooperate and hold dialogue for betterment of themselves, their businesses and also to participate in charities and social works through golf.

In the background, the book provides ample materials on Vietnamese culture and introduces leaders who achieved famous status such as Trần Hưng Đạo, who defeated mighty Mongol armies, is worshipped in Việt Nam and revered in Japan and known as one of the best generals of the century. The female general Bùi Thị Xuân was one of the rare kinds of her gender who rose up for justice and left remarkable traits.

Also lighter topics of embroidery and dress are covered with a number of photographs of beautiful *áo dài*, the traditional costume for Vietnamese women, presented along with elucidation of their salient features.

Book cover photos

Minh Hiền (Hien Minh Thi Tran) at *Chùa Một Cột*, Hà Nội, Việt Nam, 1993.

Trí Tri (Tri Tri Tran) at the the University of Tasmania gym, 1980.

Minh Trí (Tri Minh Tran), Hobart, 1983.

Trí Tuệ (Tri Tue Tran) at Hoiana Shores Golf Course, Hội An, Việt Nam.

Sunrise at Tam Thanh Beach, Tam Kỳ, Việt Nam, 13 September 2023.

Chùa Một Cột - *The One Pillar Temple*

Historical records show that one night, King Lý Thái Tông dreamed *Phật Bà Quan Âm*, Lady Buddha (also known as The Goddess of Mercy), sat on a lotus. The King consulted for its meaning with his wise council then ordered a temple resembling the lotus flower to be built in honour of *Phật Bà Quan Âm*.

The temple was named *Liên Hoa Đài, Lotus Flower Temple*. However, it is better known as *Chùa Một Cột, One Pillar Temple*, for it was built on top of one single pillar. The *One Pillar Temple* stood solemnly for centuries until the time the French left Hà Nội in 1954. The current temple was rebuilt in 1955.

The Lotus flower is a *spiritual symbol of Buddhism* because of its five characteristics:

1- *Purity*: Lotus flowers rise and bloom above dark and muddy places.
2- *Cleansing*: The muddy water pond becomes fresher because of the lotus flowers.
3- *Gentleness*: Lotus flowers' fragrance is elegant, light and mild.
4- *Resilience*: Lotus flowers undergo a long process from their early stages lying deeply beneath the mud until emerging from the water to encounter the sun.
5- *Reincarnation*: After a blossom season, lotus flowers wither then new flowers come back the next season.

The lotus flower is Việt Nam's national flower that signifies purity, serenity, cleansing, and resilience. Lotus flowers rise above the muddy water each morning, close petals in the afternoon and sink beneath the water's surface during the night. Hence it is also known as the flower of the dawn. Though born from mud and submerged underwater every evening, lotus flowers remain pristine.

The white lotus represents purity, grace, peacefulness and faith. The blue lotus symbolises wisdom and logic. The purple lotus connotes spirituality. The centre of the lotus flowers is either a yellow or yellowish-green hue. Yellow is the colour of gold that signifies achievement of all enlightenment and, green is the colour of rebirth.

The pink lotus represents devotion to Lord Buddha.

Lotus flowers are planted in the pond in the front of every ancestral house, in temples and in lakes throughout Việt Nam.

About the Author

Minh Hiền is an educator, a researcher and the author of *The Vietnamese Australians: Traditions, Education, Tenacity* and *My Heritage: Vietnam fatherland motherland*.

Minh Hiền at her Hobart home reviewing her book while watching the Royal Princess, November 2023.

She was selected to participate in the 2023 Queensland Writers Centre (QWC) short-listed *Publishable* program and was long-listed in the QWC *Publishable* program in 2022, the 2021 *Fellowship & Access Manuscript Development* initiative through the QWC, the 2019 *Hardcopy* National Professional Development Program initiative through the ACT Writers Centre to write her memoir.

In 2006, she was awarded an Australian Society of Authors Mentorship and was mentored by Judith Lukin-Amundsen while completing a Master of Arts in Creative Writing.

She has worked as an engineer, an IT consultant, a systems accountant, a systems manager and a family business manager and owner. While working, she studied for university qualifications in the fields of Engineering, Accounting, Commerce, Management, Arts, and Education and has a qualification as a professional member of the Australian Society of Certified Practising Accountants (CPA).

She holds a Master of Education, a Master of Higher Education, a Master of Arts in Creative Writing, a Master of Commerce, a Master of Engineering Science, a Graduate Diploma in Management, a Graduate Conversion Course qualification in Accounting and a Bachelor of Engineering with Honours from universities in NSW, VIC, QLD and TAS. She is featured in the 2008 *Who's Who in Tasmania*.

Minh Hiền visits the Xá Lợi Temple, Chùa Xá Lợi, Sài Gòn, September 2023.

Minh Hiền visits the pine tree at the river in front of her Sydney home, October 2023.

The Vietnamese Australians: Heritage and Contributions by Minh Hiền

Our Heritage

For thousands of years, despite facing war and poverty, the Vietnamese were content with their lives in their own country. Whether following traditions, or believing in compassion, the Vietnamese care for their elders and love their motherland.

With deep roots in ancestral worship, most Vietnamese, who moved outside their family home to study or to work, would return home every *Tết*, the Vietnamese New Year. Those who were educated overseas would return to Việt Nam once they completed their studies.

According to the Australian Bureau of Statistics records, prior to the Fall of Saigon in 1975, there were about 700 Vietnam-born people in Australia.[1]

This changed drastically between 1975 and 1985.

On 30 April 1975, the Communist North took over Sài Gòn, the capital city of the former South Vietnamese government. Millions of Vietnamese left their country in small fishing boats.

In Malaysia, to deter the Vietnamese refugees from landing on their islands the government of Malaysia ordered the police to shoot at any unwanted boats coming up on its beaches. As a result, many ships and crews refused to rescue people on sinking boats, for they had nowhere to unload them.

Wooden Refugee Boats crowded with men, women and children in heavy seas. Thuyền Nhân Việt Nam, watercolour painting on paper by Ellyse Tran in 2023.

Thousands starved or drowned in the Pacific Ocean. Numerous media reports on the condition of the Vietnamese refugees referred to them as 'boat people' and compared their hopeless situation with the Holocaust victims. These reports shocked the United Nations High Commissioner for Refugees (UNHCR) and people in the US, Canada, Australia, France, West Germany, the UK, etc.

In 1978, the Australian government removed from official policy all migrant selection criteria based on country of origin and announced it would honour its obligations to the Vietnamese refugees, stating that the Vietnamese exodus was the result of a conflict in which Australia had been a party. The Frazer government abolished the White Australia Policy to honour its responsibilities due to its involvement in the Việt Nam War.

In 1982, the government allowed relatives of Vietnamese Australians to migrate to Australia under the Orderly Departure Program.

The Vietnamese immigration peaked in the late 1980s. The majority had immigrated under Australia's family reunion scheme.

The Vietnamese brought to Australia their heritage and traditions. One of the traditions is practising *Vietnamese Martial Arts*.

The *Vietnamese Martial Arts* started at least two thousand years ago in North Việt Nam. My eldest brother had been practising it since he was nine years old.

Vietnamese Martial Arts

Vietnamese Martial Arts, Việt Võ, has a strong philosophical base that was built on a long and cohesive cultural tradition stretching back to ancient times.

Việt Nam is a small country with small-built people who often had to fight against powerful invaders. Hence, the philosophy of the Vietnamese Martial Arts has been built upon the foundation of weakness against strength, minority against majority, short against tall. As a result, Việt Võ masters have developed many techniques that are simple but effective, agile and unpredictable to attack the opponent and many defence techniques that are discreet, tight and realistic.

Historians have recorded that Vietnamese Martial Arts had advanced to the same status as literature in the national school system during the Trần Dynasty in the 13th century when the Royal University for Martial Arts, *Giảng Võ Đường*, opened to train military leaders and imperial members. At the Giảng Võ Đường famous generals shared their experiences of real battlefields[2].

The martial arts examinations did not start until 1721 during the reign of King Lê Dụ Tông also known as King Bảo Thái. During that period, Giáo thụ, mandarins in charge of education in a town, were appointed to monitor the martial arts education with a specific curriculum called Military Classics[2].

In 1723, new teaching methods, called Võ Học, martial studies, were introduced to teach students with exams and under strict rules and regulations. The martial arts exams were then held every three years[2].

Saint Trần Hưng Đạo

Trần Hưng Đạo, birth name Trần Quốc Tuấn, (The Year of The Cat 1231 – The Year of The Mouse 1300) was made a Saint by the Vietnamese as he three times defeated the Mongols of the Yuan dynasty under Kublai Khan in the thirteenth century[3].

General Trần Hưng Đạo wrote a handbook on military strategy which inspired his men and they fought bravely against the invasions of the mighty Mongol armies.

The first Mongol invasion was in 1257. When the Mongols invaded Việt Nam, Trần Hưng Đạo advised the Vietnamese king and people to evacuate the city. Disease, shortage of supplies, the climate, and Trần Hưng Đạo's strategy of scorched earth tactics foiled the Mongols' invasions.

The second Mongol invasion was in 1284. Mongolian general Kublai Khan demanded passage through northern Việt Nam for his Yuan army on their invasion of the kingdom of Champa. When the Vietnamese Emperor Trần Nhân Tông refused, Mongolian Prince Toghan led an army, attacked Việt Nam and seized the capital Thăng Long (now Hà Nội). General Trần Hưng Đạo escorted the Royal Court, staying just ahead of the Mongol army. While Emperor Trần Nhân Tông withdrew from the capital, in the surrounding provinces soldiers put up posters to encourage people to resist the invaders by all means and, if necessary, to take refuge in the jungles and mountains. After burning off most of their crops and facilities, the Vietnamese retreated. When the Mongol army had been worn down by tropical diseases and lack of supplies, General Trần Hưng Đạo launched a counter-offensive. Most of the battles were on the waterfronts, where the Mongols could not use their cavalry strength. Mongol commander Sogetu of the Southern front was killed in the battle. In their withdrawal from Việt Nam, the Mongols were also attacked by the Hmong and Yao minorities in the Northern regions.

The third Mongol invasion was in 1287 when 300,000 Mongolians were defeated by the Vietnamese under the leadership of General Trần Hưng Đạo. Applying a tactic used by Ngô Quyền in 938 to defeat an invading Chinese fleet, under the leadership of General Trần Hưng Đạo, the Vietnamese drove iron-tipped stakes into the bed of the Bạch Đằng River (located in northern Việt Nam in present-day Hà Bắc, Hải Hưng, and Quảng Ninh provinces) then lured the Mongol fleet into the river just as the tide was starting to ebb. They were trapped and impaled by the iron-tipped stakes. The entire Mongol fleet was destroyed. The Mongol fleet admiral Omar was captured and executed. The Mongol army retreated to China. The ground forces of Prince Toghan were ambushed along the road through Nội Bàng, but managed to escape back to China.

Việt Nam was the only nation to defeat the Mongols whose armies swept out of remote Northern Asia on horse cavalry and briefly ruled most of modern-day Russia, China, Korea, Persia, India, the Middle East, Eastern Europe and into present day Poland and Germany. In 1984, historians from around the world, who met in London, nominated Trần Hưng Đạo as one of the top ten generals in world history[4].

With deep roots in ancestral worship, the Vietnamese governments for centuries have built statues of Trần Hưng Đạo facing the sea in all major cities. The Statue of Trần Hưng Đạo in Sài Gòn, opposite the Bạch Đằng wharf, has special meaning for most Vietnamese who left Việt Nam by boat during the 1970s and 1980s. These Vietnamese believed that Saint Trần Hưng Đạo pointing his finger to the sea means that he gave his blessing to them to leave Việt Nam and they would be safe if they prayed and asked for his protection. Many Vietnamese visit the Statue of Trần Hưng Đạo to pay respect or to pray for his blessing. In September 2023, when my husband and I visited the statue in Sài Gòn, within twenty minutes we saw three individuals riding motorbikes on a busy street who stopped at the Statue. They brought fruit, flowers and incense. They burned incense and prayed.

Minh Hiền visits the Statue of Saint Trần Hưng Đạo in Sài Gòn, September 2023.

The Vietnamese Australians: Heritage and Contributions by Minh Hiền

The Vietnamese Australians: Heritage and Contributions by Minh Hiền   p.5

Quang Trung Nguyễn Huệ

Quang Trung Nguyễn Huệ (1753-1792) was born in Tây Sơn, Bình Định. He was a descendant of the Hồ[5]. During the 18th century, Việt Nam was divided into two parts. Chúa (Lord) Trịnh ruled the North and Chúa Nguyễn ruled the South. They held all the power. The figurehead was King Lê (of the later Lê dynasty) who was under total control of Lord Trịnh in the capital Thăng Long.

A young farmer and Martial Artist, named *Nguyễn Huệ*, secretly organised his army in the jungles and mountains then fought with the big ambition of reuniting the country. Historians recorded it as the *Tây Sơn rebellion*. King Lê Chiêu Thống sent envoys to the Imperial court of the Qing Empire in China asking for aid to fight against the *Tây Sơn*. China sent large troops to Việt Nam and captured the capital Thăng Long[5].

Nguyễn Huệ's troops retreated to the South and refused to engage the Qing army. He raised a large army of his own and defeated the invader on the Lunar New Year's Eve of 1789. King Lê Chiêu Thống and the imperial family fled Việt Nam into China and never returned. The Lê dynasty ended after ruling Việt Nam for 356 years[5].

Nguyễn Huệ called himself, Bình Định Vương, which means "The King who had pacified the country." King Nguyễn Huệ, also known as *Emperor Quang Trung*, came from Bình Định, a small town in Central Việt Nam[5].

The Statue of Quang Trung in Quy Nhơn, September 2023.

Most Vietnamese Martial Arts schools from this region called *Võ Bình Định*, Bình Định Martial Arts that have a fearsome reputation due to Bình Định being the birthplace of many talented heroic people: Nguyễn Nhạc, Nguyễn Huệ, Nguyễn Lữ, Lady Bùi Thị Xuân, Võ Văn Dũng and Trần Quang Diệu.

Bình Định is known as the cradle of the powerful Vietnamese Martial Arts where most men and women learnt martial arts. It was Quang Trung's birthplace and due to his victories over China and his success in unifying Việt Nam, there are museums and statues of him in this province.

The Vietnamese Australians: Heritage and Contributions by Minh Hiền

The Quang Trung museum in Bình Định, September 2023.

Quang Trung Nguyễn Huệ's parents' well in the Quang Trung Museum.

Bùi Thị Xuân

Bùi Thị Xuân was a Vietnamese female general during the *Tây Sơn rebellion*. She was one of the five principal women during the Tây Sơn Dynasty. According to historians, she had learnt martial arts since she was a child. She was a very strong and brave woman. She fought enemies using the *song kiếm* double sword; she also rode horses and shot with a bow[6]. Vietnamese history books recorded that General Bùi Thị Xuân's special talent was her excellent abilities in training women and elephants to fight in battles. She trained 5,000 women and 200 elephants and led them into battles and won[6].

Bùi Thị Xuân was the General Commander of Elephant Troops, the present day equivalent of Tanks General Commander. After Tây Sơn lost to the Nguyễn, she was captured and executed by being crushed under elephants' feet.

Legend has it that before the execution, she was calm as if she was about to go to a tea party.

The governor of the jail asked her what was her last wish.

She said that she wanted a long piece of fabric to wrap around her body as she didn't want her flesh to be showed in public after she was trampled by elephants.

He granted her wish.

After she wrapped her whole body with extra clothes, she walked with her head high to face the elephants in the execution yard. (This was similar to Gladiators fighting with Lions in Roman times, but she wasn't allowed to fight).

The two elephants, despite nudging and poking with sharp sticks from their handlers, refused to step forward to crush her. She smiled faintly and loudly, ordered the two elephants to charge forward and crush her.

Vietnamese governments, post- and pre- 1975 eras, named schools and streets after her. There is a large temple in her birthplace in Bình Định.

The Bùi Thị Xuân's temple in Bình Định, September 2023.

In *Võ Bình Định*, there is a *Double Swords Pattern* called *Nữ Tướng (Female General) Bùi Thị Xuân's Kiếm Pháp* and, there is a famous Vietnamese jingle:

> *Ai về Bình Định mà coi,*
> *Con gái Bình Định múa roi, đi quyền.*

> Let's come to Bình Định to watch,
> The women perform martial arts.

During the 19th century, Việt Nam was occupied by France. At this time there were many Vietnamese resistance groups. These groups were at a disadvantage in comparison with the French soldiers since they had very little modern weaponry and the strict rules imposed by the French prohibited the Vietnamese from carrying swords.

In this situation, the Vietnamese resistance groups were trained to use bamboo sticks to fight and most of them had been taught Bình Định Martial Arts. Because of this Vietnamese Martial Arts has placed a lot of emphasis on Đao Pháp and Côn Pháp (The use of broad-sword and long staff).

During the colonial period, Vietnamese Martial Arts were taught in family schools only, from father to son. Its study was kept secret, with students promising to never use their martial arts without serious reason and to not divulge its secrets.

These days, many people consider Việt Võ training like a sport.

In September 2023, on a visit to the Quang Trung museum at Nguyễn Huệ's birthplace, fifty kilometres from Quy Nhơn, the capital city of *Bình Định*, we watched 'con gái Bình Định múa roi, đi quyền'.

A woman performs martial arts at the Quang Trung museum, September 2023.

The Vietnamese Education System

The Vietnamese education system has its roots in Ancestor Worship, Buddhism and Confucianism. Pior to the 1970s, teachers and parents imparted knowledge of respect for elders to the younger generation and taught them five virtues: *Nhân, Lễ, Nghĩa, Trí, Tín* - Benevolence, Propriety, Righteousness, Wisdom and Trustworthiness.

Vietnamese girls were educated at home in the four virtues: *Công, Dung, Ngôn, Hạnh* - Diligence, Elegance, Proper Speech and Good Behaviour.

Virtue 'Công' meant that Vietnamese girls were taught cooking as well as needle-work such as embroidery and sewing from an early age. They were expected to be able to cook, to make clothes and to embroider handkerchiefs, clothes, artefacts for people they loved or cared for.

> Living in Australia, many of these Vietnamese women applied their needle-work expertise by making clothes at home for their community and the wider Australian community in order to earn money to support their families. Many women also applied their cooking training to earn a living, by working in cafés or restaurants. Some worked side-by-side with their husbands at their food or clothing family business which often operated from home.

Virtue 'Dung' meant that Vietnamese girls were taught to dress modestly, elegantly and beautifully.

> The Vietnamese national dress, *áo dài*, has been worn by girls and women since ancient times for all occasions and for all ages.

> There are various styles of áo dài. The current most popular style was designed in the 1930s to suit 'modern' Vietnamese women who expected to work at home as well as outside their homes.

> My mother, an áo dài maker for all her life, explained to me that: "A beautifully made áo dài with embroidery is a piece of art that shows the core characteristics of the woman who wears it. The áo dài with embroidery shows that a Vietnamese woman of the twentieth century is not just an obedient daughter, a faithful wife, a devoted mother but also a gracious and dignified individual who not only has *Công, Dung, Ngôn, Hạnh* but also works professionally to support her family."

Virtue 'Ngôn' meant that Vietnamese girls were taught to speak softly, politely and use deferential language.

Virtue 'Hạnh' meant that Vietnamese girls were taught respect, integrity, trustworthiness and piety.

Pre-1970s, a Vietnamese woman was expected to look after her home, to make sacrifices for her husband and children. Her mother and her father's mother were her teachers, if she was fortunate to have them both. Otherwise, her aunties were her teachers.

The Vietnamese Australians: Heritage and Contributions by Minh Hiền

Minh Hiền, Sydney, August 1988.

Minh Hiền, Tân Sơn Nhất airport, Sài Gòn, 1992.

Minh Hiền in her áo dài during the 1990s.

Minh Hiền in her áo dài in September 2023.

The Vietnamese Australians: Heritage and Contributions by Minh Hiền

I had watched my mother making clothes since I was born till the day I left Việt Nam in a fishing boat. Whenever my mother made a new blouse or a new áo dài, she explained why she had chosen a certain colour, why she had made a certain style and why they looked good on me. Even today, I can hear her melodious voice:

> *White symbolises purity, grace and innocence,*
> *Pink is for girls,*
> *Blue is the colour of trust for sky blue and generosity for dark blue,*
> *Green is the colour of tenacity,*
> *Purple is the colour of royalty and nobility,*
> *Red is the colour of the five-fingered flower – the flower of love,*
> *Orange is the colour of the sun – the sun of honesty,*
> *Yellow is the colour of gold – gold for people – the people of loyalty.*
> *Be like the Sunflower – always turning towards the sun - the sun of truth, loyalty and honesty.*
> *Be like the Lotus flower– though born from mud and submerged underwater every evening, always remain pristine: showing purity, serenity, cleanliness and resilience.*
> *The Chrysanthemum flower symbolises gratitude, resilience, longevity and fidelity.*
> *The Peacock symbolises wealth, beauty, openness and dignity and is associated with an earthly form of the Phoenix.*

While I was living in Hobart and my mother was in Sài Gòn, she made me many embroidered blouses. She sent them, one by one, in a brown-paper envelope via post. She made me a number of blue blouses embroidered with blue sunflowers. She made me various red blouse with red roses delicately strung as a garland in the shape of the heart.

My mother especially loved the colour purple and sunflowers. In 1981, when I received my new blouse from my mother, I spread it on my bed and ran my fingers over the silken threads. It had short puff sleeves and a round neck. There were eight large sunflowers, eight buds and fourteen leaves. Each flower centred with numerous seeds of red, surrounded by large petals in bright orange and shining yellow. When I touched the silken purple, I saw my mother bending her head over a piece of fabric, holding it carefully with her left hand while up and down her right hand moved, pulling a tiny needle with a long thread, little by little, the needle leaving a tiny trace of red, orange, yellow, green.

Minh Hiền in her purple blouse, Hobart, 1988.

The Vietnamese Australians: Heritage and Contributions by Minh Hiền

Minh Hiền at her Hobart home in Albion Heights, 1993.

Minh Hiền at her Hobart home in Albion Heights, Moon and Sun rise, November 2023.

Even these days, the influences of Ancestor Worship, Buddhism and Confucianism are strong within the Vietnamese education system, especially in rural areas and small towns. Teachers and parents still impart knowledge of respect for elders to the younger generation and girls still learn the four virtues: *Công, Dung, Ngôn, Hạnh* - Diligence, Elegance, Proper Speech and Good Behaviour.

Virtue 'Công' means that Vietnamese girls are taught to learn to cook as well as to work outside their home. They are expected to be able to earn money to be independent and to support their families and elderly parents. Their parents and teachers often encourage them to learn English at school and university. As a result, many Vietnamese girls from rural areas or small towns are inspired to become an English teacher or a tour guide.

Virtue 'Dung' means that Vietnamese girls are taught to dress modestly. Many girls still wear *áo dài* when they attend classes. However, they are no longer taught that "a beautifully made *áo dài* with embroidery is a piece of art that shows the core characteristics of the woman who wears it." Because, nowadays, very few people know how to embroider.

Virtue 'Ngôn' still means that Vietnamese girls are taught to speak softly and politely.

Virtue 'Hạnh' still means that Vietnamese girls are taught respect, integrity, trustworthiness and piety.

Nowadays, a good Vietnamese woman still makes sacrifices for her husband and children.

Minh Hiền with her final-year online students and their class teacher (cô chủ nhiệm) Diệu Hiền at the Quang Nam University, Tam Kỳ, Việt Nam, September 2023.

The Vietnamese Australians: Heritage and Contributions by Minh Hiền

Minh Hiền with her third-year online students, Tam Kỳ, Việt Nam, September 2023.

Minh Hiền with her second-year online students, Tam Kỳ, Việt Nam, September 2023.

Our Stories of Coming to Australia

My parents had worked extremely hard to bring us up during the war in Việt Nam, to survive the harsh life after the Fall of Saigon and to get us to Australia by boat.

Tri Tri Tran is my eldest brother. His name in Vietnamese is Trần Trí Tri.

Tri Tue Tran is my second-elder brother. His name in Vietnamese is Trần Trí Tuệ.

Tri Minh Tran is my younger brother. His name in Vietnamese is Trần Minh Trí.

Even though their names are different in spellings, all have the same meanings.

Trần is our surname which is the second most popular Vietnamese surname because the Trần dynasty was one of the most prosperous dynasties in Vietnamese history.

The Vietnamese considers people's middle name and first name together as one name.

Trí Tri, Trí Tuệ and Minh Trí share the same meanings: Intelligence and Wisdom.

When my mother gave birth to my eldest brother Trí Tri, the war in Việt Nam between the North and the South had just started.

My father had come to the South from a village in the North and my mother was born in a village in the South.

My parents just wanted peace.

My father's philosophy was that in order to achieve peace and development all men must have intelligence and wisdom.

Thus, my parents named my eldest brother, *Trí Tri,* my second-elder brother *Trí Tuệ* and my younger brother *Minh Trí.*

My eldest brother, Trí Tri, arrived in Tasmania in the Year of the Goat 1979, from a refugee camp in Malaysia. Tri had tried to escape Việt Nam three times. At home in Sài Gòn, for many weeks we tensely awaited news from Tri. It was quite a while before we received a letter from him. Years later I learnt that his tiny boat of thirty-one people was fired at by Malaysian police, the leaking and broken boat had washed ashore on a deserted island in Malaysia and his time in the ocean had been filled with tragedy until the UNHCR intervened, but Tri never wrote any details of his hardship or loneliness. All his letters home were full of love.

My second elder brother, Trí Tuệ, arrived in Tasmania in the Year of the Monkey 1980, also from a refugee camp in Malaysia. Tuệ had made a few false attempts to escape Việt Nam before his final escape. Pirates attacked his boat twice. The first group of pirates took all the gold from everyone. When the second group came, they strip-searched people for gold but found nothing, they pulled an old man's gold-plated tooth out. Tuệ, like Tri, only wrote home about happy events.

A year after Tuệ left, the Head of our local People's Community Office summoned my younger brother, Minh Trí, to his office. Two years earlier, the government had sent some leaders to live on the Northern borders to keep order. Now, the government was planning to send every able-bodied young man to the North for military service.

Minh Trí, at home we called him Bé, was only fourteen years old. But our local People's Community Office wanted to make sure they got his name so as to be ready to call him up if the war with China escalated further.

As my father made plans to send Bé away, he remembered when Việt Nam was divided in the 1950s, he had to leave his parents in a village in the North. He had thought he would be away for just a few years, but he never saw his parents again. Now, he thought we should all leave Việt Nam. But he could not make up his mind. For many days, he was so deep in thought that twice he walked out into the street in his pyjamas.

One day, someone told my father about *lên đồng*, a custom that had been practised by many Vietnamese since ancient times. It was about the living consulting with someone who could communicate with people from the other world through prayers.

With a history of war for many centuries, all Vietnamese families suffered human losses. *Lên đồng* was one of the ways for them to grieve and to move on with life because many Vietnamese believe that when their family members die their spirits live.

Many Vietnamese, especially people of my parents and elders' generation, believe that when their parents pass away the parents continue to watch over them and their children. Most Vietnamese have a family altar in their home where on the anniversary of their loved ones' passing away *ngày giỗ* and on special occasions such as *Tết*, the Vietnamese New Year, they lay special food there and burn incense inviting their loved ones' spirits home.

My father did not believe in lên đồng but he told my mother about it.

My mother said, 'Why don't we ask your parents and my father what we should do?'

As the eldest son of my grandparents, my father felt it was his duty to visit his parents' graves and his ancestral village, but he had had no opportunity and now, if he left Việt Nam, he would never fulfil that duty.

My mother was also thinking of visiting her own village and her father's grave.

My parents decided to see a lên đồng woman. At the entrance of her house, my parents were led into a passage where they smelled incense and heard the chanting of prayers. They tiptoed into a small room, and then the door was closed behind them. Thick bamboo curtains across the windows blocked all light from outside. Oil lamps and candles lit the room dimly. About ten people were sitting on a bamboo mat on the floor in a semi-circle. In the middle a woman knelt in prayer in front of an altar covered in flowers, fruit, lighted candles and burning incense.

Everyone was silent while the lên đồng woman was chanting prayers. The lên đồng woman turned to a man and talked to him for a while then turned away and chanted another prayer.

The woman abruptly turned to my father. Her eyes were closed while her head and body rocked slightly. She asked if he would like to ask the spirit a question.

'How should I address you?' My father decided to test the woman.

'You call me U, son,' the woman said.

My father froze.

Her voice and the way she said U stunned him.

For more than twenty-five years, he had not uttered this sound, this word. He had not told anyone even my mother that he used to call his mother U.

How could this woman know that I called my mother U? He thought.

'Why haven't you returned to the village, son?' The woman spoke as if she were his U. 'But never mind,' the woman added after a moment, 'I know you sent money to rebuild Thầy and U's graves. That is good enough, son. No need to make a special trip to the village. Thầy and U are living comfortably here. You need not worry.'

Then, as if she had read his mind, she added, 'Ah, yes, you want to talk to Thầy. Yes, you can call him up. Don't hesitate! You can call Thầy up now, son.'

The question my father had intended to ask, and had not mentioned to anyone, this woman had answered, not even waiting for him to voice it. He was dumbfounded.

The woman turned away, chanted another prayer, then again turned to my father. In a booming voice, she called out, 'Ah! So, that was you! I was on my way to the temple and you disturbed me! You have never burned any incense for me at home. Why are you coming here to call me up?'

My father was petrified. Later when I asked him about his consultation, he could not remember the rest of what his father said through the woman.

When the woman had finished saying another set of prayers, she turned to my father and said in a quiet voice, 'I did not go a natural way, son.'

This time my father realised that the spirit who was speaking to him was his uncle. He had loved this uncle dearly. His uncle was poisoned to death in the 1950s when his ancestral village was occupied by the Communist North troops.

'Who killed you?' He asked a question which he had in his mind for twenty-five years.

'Don't ask me that question, son. It is dangerous. Don't look at the past. Look to the future, son.'

'Is there anything do you wish me to do?' He asked.

'When you see my children, tell them to burn incense for me. They never did.'

Later, when my father told his uncle's daughter, auntie Phương, about that message, her face went white. Auntie Phương said that she and her siblings had not burned any incense for their father for some twenty-five years. After that, every year and to this day, on her father's Memorial Day, auntie Phương cooks a special meal and burns incense for him.

The woman turned towards the altar and chanted another prayer. Then she turned to my mother. 'Your two sons,' she said as if she were my mother's father, 'they did not let me rest! But, don't you worry about them, they are good boys.' She spoke for a while. Some of the things that she spoke were known only by my mother and her siblings.

When I asked my father, he explained that his intention had been to check out the lên đồng woman. If she was believable then he would tell her to tell his U that if he left Vietnam, he would never be able to return to the village and visit her grave. But he did not know how he would tell her because he was afraid others, hearing him, would report him to the police.

'How could she know I call my mother U? How could she know that my uncle was murdered? I didn't say anything and yet that woman told me, "You need not go back to the village, son." And the way she spoke, I felt as if she were my U.' Papa's voice was shaking as he recalled it.

My father explained that he understood the message to mean, 'Leave, son. You need not go back to the village, son. Leave now.'

By that time tension was running high between Vietnam and China.

The government of Vietnam loaded hundreds of thousands of people of Chinese origin onto a large ship and sent them out into the Pacific Ocean. Many Vietnamese disguised themselves as Chinese Vietnamese to board these ships to escape Vietnam. Someone introduced my father to a man who knew the officials who were organising one such ship. My father's friends said that it was safer than escaping on small fishing boats and they wanted to send their families out of Vietnam in one of these large ships. None of us was of Chinese origin. My father paid the officials to get necessary papers and twenty-five places on board.

A few weeks later, our family and five other families were sitting in small groups, along the streets from the Bến Thành Market to Nhà Hát Lớn, the French-built Opera House in central Sài Gòn. My father's friend, Mr Xiêm, and my father's former French teacher sat in front of the Opera House. The organiser allowed each group to take one or two relatives onto the wharf, and these relatives would stand on the dock and wave.

While waiting, suddenly my father felt nervous. He stood up and walked to one of the organisers and said, 'Let us board the ship last.'

I sat with Bình, a daughter of Papa's friend, watching the activities in the busy street. My spirit was high as I was thinking that we would board a grand ship to go abroad. My mind drifted back and forth to some of the things that had happened to our family in the past few years.

When the nearby clock struck ten, my father felt troubled. He said to his friend and his former teacher, 'I've a strange feeling that bothers me. I do not know what it is or how to describe it, but my sixth sense tells me that this is not a good move.'

'You make the decision,' his friend said.

'If you say go, we go. If you say stay, we stay.' My father's former teacher added.

'Let me think,' my father said. 'Please leave me alone for a few minutes.'

He then stood up and began to walk away from them.

He did not think. He moved like a sleepwalker.

Later, he said to me that he did not plan to act that way and he could not remember what was in his mind at the time, only that his legs carried him towards my direction.

He stopped in front of me while facing the street.

'Go home,' he whispered, without looking at me.

I turned and said quietly to Bình, 'Let us go home!'

Bình relayed the same message to others in her group.

In less than five minutes twenty-five people received the message and all quietly went home. We left in small groups of three as if we had just gone out for a night of sight-seeing.

The following morning, before dawn, some of the twenty-five people came to our home, wanted to know why my father had decided not to allow us to proceed to the wharf.

'My cousin saw everyone boarding the ship except us,' Bình lamented. 'Why didn't you let us go?'

'I don't know why,' my father said, looking confused.

While we were gathered in our living room, the wife of my father's contact rushed in and burst into tears.

'They cheated us!' she screamed. 'They took our money. They stripped off all the gold that people carried, loaded everyone on trucks then drove them to the Chí Hòa Prison.'

She sobbed. 'The police came to our house this morning for my husband. Do you know anyone who can help me to get him out of prison?'

The people who boarded that ship were the first one thousand or so to be trapped by the government with its new and secret policy. All were imprisoned, some up to five years. A year or so earlier, when the government had sent a shipload of people of Chinese origin out to sea, they had been criticised and pressured by other Western countries. The government had then changed its policy and sent these people to be brainwashed in an isolated camp instead. The giant ship, which we were about to board, was the first ship that government officials used to lure people onto the wharf. They allowed relatives to come to the wharf to say goodbye. After the relatives went away, the officials stripped the people, searching for their gold and jewellery then sent them initially to prison, later to re-education camps in remote forest areas.

My parents had lost a lot of gold to arrange for us to leave on that ship. They were distressed about our loss and felt for those in prison. But it did not take long for my father to pick himself up and try again. After two attempts as a whole family, my mother told him to concentrate on sending only my younger brother Bé away.

By this time the war with China had escalated.

The worries entered my father's mind, 'What would his daughters' future be and with whom would they marry when all the good and capable boys had gone?'

Because I was the eldest daughter, my father wanted to send me away with Bé. He discussed this with his friends who had daughters of my age before he made the decision.

Bé and I arrived in Tasmania in the Year of the Rooster 1981, from a refugee camp in Singapore. We had made numerous false escapes together before we made the real escape from Bà Rịa. When we were in a small fishing boat and the sea became violent, Bé encouraged me. He collected water and food for me.

We were very lucky that we were rescued by the *USS John Young*.

The USS John Young.
Oil painting on canvas by Ellyse Tran in 2021.

The UNHCR reported that 349 boats out of 452 from Việt Nam headed for Thailand had been attacked by Thai pirates, with 578 women raped and 228 kidnapped. As a result of this report, the UNHCR established a strategy to stop and arrest pirates[7].

The UNHCR was awarded the 1981 Nobel Peace Prize for its work in setting up refugee camps in Malaysia, Thailand, the Philippines, Hong Kong and Indonesia to process the 'boat people'[7].

By 1981, 49,616 Vietnamese had been resettled in Australia[1].

In 1982, the Orderly Departure Program allowed relatives of Vietnamese Australians to migrate to Australia.

In 1986, my parents migrated to Hobart, Tasmania, under Australia's Family Reunion scheme.

That same year, the Vietnamese government instituted a new policy called *Đổi Mới*, Economic Renewal.

As a result, many Vietnamese from Australia started visiting their relatives and investing in industries in their motherland.

Việt Nam has since changed drastically.

In September 2023, I revisited the corner of the street where my father whispered to me: 'Go home'.

It has completely changed.

In the mornings, wealthy middle-aged men and women stop their bicycles and do exercise.

In the evenings, young people play live music in the park opposite the Opera House.

Minh Hiền, Sài Gòn, September 2023.

Our Contributions

This chapter is about our contributions to Australia through education and sport.

Education

When I was born, my father was separated from his parents due to the war. Remembering my grandfather's philosophy, my father named me *Minh Hiền*.

In English, the meaning of my name is 'one should use both head and heart'.

Using my head, I like learning. Using my heart, I like teaching and helping others to progress through education.

I started teaching others when I was in junior high school, in Australia, five months after my arrival.

The night before I left my childhood home, my father whispered: *Leave, daughter. Without an education you have no future... Don't abandon your studies. No one can take away your understanding and your knowledge, but cruel people can take away your money and position.*

Minh Hiền at the Singapore Refugee Camp, 1981.

When I arrived in Hobart, Tasmania, in 1981, I wanted to get a university qualification.

I had eight months to learn English before I could enrol for Matriculation the following year. I had studied English as a subject for a few years at high school. After the fall of Saigon, English was discouraged and I never had a chance to speak English with Westerners until I was in the refugee camp.

In Hobart, I had no friends to talk to and there were no English classes for a few weeks after I arrived. So my eldest brother Tri asked Sister Anne, a Catholic nun, whom he met through his job, to teach me English at home while I was waiting for a proper English class.

A few weeks later I attended a formal English class.

My teacher, Mrs Margaret Eldridge, was a well-built and tall English woman with a caring face. Considering that I was a tiny girl, she looked like a giant. She had an equally big and kind heart as I found out later. She was the teacher-in-charge of the English language program at Mount St Canice Migrant Hostel where most of the Vietnamese refugees who first came to Hobart lived. She inspired confidence in me to learn English.

After the ten-week course with Margaret, I studied English at evening classes for a few weeks at the Adult Migrant Education Centre in a building next to the State Library.

The Vietnamese Australians: Heritage and Contributions by Minh Hiền

One day in November 1981, Tri came back from work and said, 'Do you want to teach?'

'Teach whom?' I asked.

'The head of the Migrant Resource Centre (MRC), Mrs Elizabeth Liu, asked me if I knew someone who could teach high school students Mathematics and Science. I could not think of anyone better than you.'

> I had shown my studious nature since I was at primary school. When I was in fifth grade, I often came to Tri with lots of questions. One day, he gave me a very thick book and said that the answers to my questions were in the book. When I asked him for the page number, he said he did not remember which page it was. He thought that would keep me away from him for a few weeks. However a few days later I told him the answers and that I had finished reading the whole book.

> When Sài Gòn fell, my mother's sister was very poor as her husband was not allowed to work because he was the principal of a school prior to the fall of Saigon. Their small children, aged three, four and six, lived in our house. My cousins did not have residential status in Sài Gòn so they could not go to school.

I taught them every day.

I read aloud proverbs for the older ones to write down in their notebooks.

> *Công Cha như núi Thái Sơn,*
>
> *Nghĩa mẹ như nước trong nguồn chảy ra,*
>
> *Một lòng thờ mẹ kính cha,*
>
> *Cho tròn chữ hiếu, mới là đạo con.*
>
> Father's devotion is as big as mount Thái Sơn,
>
> Mother's love is like water flowing from the spring,
>
> Faithfully honour mother and respect father,
>
> To uphold filial piety is to fulfil obligations to one's parents.

I explained the meanings of the new words to them. When they made spelling mistakes, I corrected them.

For the younger ones, I sang an alphabet poem and they repeated after me:

> *O tròn như qủa trứng gà,*
>
> *Ô thì đội mũ,*
>
> *Ơ thì thêm râu.*
>
> Letter O is as round as a hen's egg.
>
> Letter Ô wears a hat,
>
> Letter Ơ has a whisker.

After the writing lessons, I taught the younger ones how to add, the older one to multiply and the smallest one to count. In the evening, I taught the neighbours kids. Later, I also taught grandchildren of my father's friend.

Now Tri said, 'Think about it. She wants the answer by the end of this week before she looks for someone else.'

'Do you think I can do it?' I asked. 'I have been in Australia for only four months and I have only finished a short course of English.'

'I do not have any doubt about your ability to teach,' Tri said. 'They are refugee students. Many are Vietnamese. Some are East Europeans. I will borrow books from the library for you to prepare lessons.'

'Ok. I will do it,' I said.

Then for the following two months, to save bus fare money, I cycled to the State Library on Tri's yellow-coloured bike. When I sat on his bike, my arms were straight and my shoulders were forward towards the handles. There was no basket in the front and no rack at the back for me to put my bag. It had the triangle frame; the top tube was horizontal, parallel to the ground, holding the seat and the handles together. I rested my bag against the top tube while gripping firmly on the bag handles with my left hand. I wore no helmet. My waist-length black hair was blowing by the gentle wind of summer as I rode along Giblin Street, turned right to Augusta Road passing Calvary Hospital, and turned right to Elizabeth Street.

I had no sense of fear about cars and buses behind me. The steep hills along some parts of the road and the sharp curve of Elizabeth Street and the stream of cars, behind me and oncoming, did not discourage me. I was young, fit and I had been riding a bicycle along busy streets in Sài Gòn since I was ten years old.

I had always loved the library atmosphere.

My spirits lifted as I walked along a row of bookshelves, I picked up high school physics, chemistry and mathematics books. I glanced through them then carried them to a large table and spread them out. To save money on photocopying, I wrote passages from the books into my notebook. I sat for hours reading and writing. I pressed the pen hard on a page of my note book. I turned page after page as I wrote lessons which I imaged that someone a few years younger than me would want to learn. I enjoyed preparing lessons for the students and I felt good about teaching young people.

It was school holidays; Elizabeth College allowed the MRC to use their classrooms.

It was a beautiful summer day. I carried my notebooks in my bag and walked with seven youths, aged between thirteen and sixteen, from the MRC to Elizabeth College. We crossed at the traffic lights then walked through a large courtyard. We climbed the wide stairways then turned into a large room with high ceiling. There were rows of desks and benches facing two large green boards on the wall. In a corner there was a large desk.

The youths sat on the first two wooden benches while I stood on the other side of the wooden desk on the first row. I laid down my notebooks and asked them what they wanted to learn. They spoke to each other in their own languages for a few minutes then a Polish girl, about fifteen years old, asked me what mathematics in Australia is like.

I showed her the lessons that I had written in my notebook.

She read it carefully then looked up and smiled.

"Same, same," she said as she passed my notebook to her friend.

The youths in the second row came over to my side and peered into my handwritten notebook.

The Vietnamese boys asked me many questions in Vietnamese.

I explained to them in English that no matter where they came from mathematics was the same.

Their eyes were sparkling.

I smiled.

Then I glanced at all the youths and said slowly, 'The very famous German Mathematician, David Hilbert, had said "Mathematics knows no races or geographic boundaries; for mathematics, the cultural world is one country".'

I was not sure if their English was adequate to understand, so I asked, 'Do you understand what I said?'

The Polish girls shook their heads.

The Vietnamese boys asked me in Vietnamese, 'What does that mean?'

I walked to the board, picked up a piece of white chalk and wrote on the green board the sentence then I told them to check the new words in their dictionary.

They got together in groups, turned the pages of their pocket dictionary and read.

After a few minutes, they all looked up at me and smiled.

My spirits lifted.

My first day of teaching Mathematics in Australia was a success.

I got paid for the hours I taught.

The payment was not much for an Australian, but it was quite a big sum for a refugee who had just arrived.

I saved every dollar that I earned to send to my parents.

Mrs Liu said that the refugee youths loved learning from me.

I got a teaching job again the following two summers.

Later, I found out that Mrs Liu received some money from the government for a Christmas party but she baked cakes at home for the party and put most of the money aside to pay for tutors to teach refugee youths rather than spending all money on cakes and drink. Her actions impressed me. I remember her until this day.

For me, that teaching experience gave me confidence that I could teach others what I knew and I have continued teaching those who wish to learn from me.

The Vietnamese Australians: Heritage and Contributions by Minh Hiền

At eighteen, I had one clear aim that I would go to university to get an education so that I could work in my chosen profession and would lead a useful and independent life.

The requirements to get to university were that I had to pass all six level-three Matriculation subjects which normally took two years to complete.

'You can enrol for five subjects,' said Tuệ in an enthusiastic voice. 'You can attend classes for two mathematics subjects, two physics subjects and one chemistry subject. You can study another mathematics subject on your own without enrolment, at the end of the year you can sit six examinations.'

Tuệ did not have any doubt that I would complete six subjects in one year, even though he himself did only four subjects. He was two years older than me and had come to Hobart eighteen months before me. As a mature-age student he was allowed to go to university when he passed four level-three matriculation subjects.

For the mathematics subject in which I did not enrol, I could use his notes to study, and if needed, I could enrol in an evening class that ran for mature adults. With Tuệ's encouragement, I enrolled for five level-three subjects but planned to matriculate with six level-three subjects at the end of that year.

Within one year of studies, I passed six Matriculation subjects with very high marks.

I was among the top five in the State. I received an award for the highest mark for the Advanced Mathematics subject.

Minh Hiền received the best mark award for Advanced Mathematics, Hobart Matriculation College, Tasmania, 1983.

On Wednesday 12 January 1983, when I was sitting in the library of the MRC, a journalist and a cameraman from the Mercury newspaper came to interview me and to take my photo.

My picture appeared on the front page of the Mercury two days later. I loved the photo on the newspaper. The Mercury did not print the names of the journalist and the photographer. I wish I knew who they were.

A few weeks later, the Examiner's journalist and photographer came to the MRC to interview me and to take my photo. A full length article about me and my achievements was published on the Examiner newspaper.

The Mercury and The Examiner, January and February 1983.

I felt great that I had achieved my goal and I had my freedom to study for an Electrical Engineering degree. I felt lucky that I could study for my chosen profession and gain work experience in my adopted country where I would live a life of freedom and peace.

While doing my undergraduate study at the University of Tasmania, I received the *H M Bamford Scholarship* from a Tasmanian engineering and electrical company which I greatly appreciated.

I graduated with Honours in 1986. I had obtained the second highest mark among all engineering students who graduated at the University of Tasmania that year.

The Mercury and the Examiner once again interviewed me about my life, my achievements and my goals.

The Sunday Tasmanian, April 1987.

Minh Hiền's graduation at the University of Tasmania, April 1987.

But, when I applied for an engineering job at the largest intercommunication company in Hobart, the senior engineer called me into his office and in front of another male engineer said that he could not offer me the job because I graduated with Honours.

A few days later I found out that he offered that job to one of my male classmates who had completed the degree with average passing grades.

I was shocked, speechless and disappointed.

At that time my mother was in the last stages of Motor Neurone Disease, she could not talk in full sentences but with great efforts she spoke one word at a time: *You do not need to work for people who do not appreciate education and devotion.*

I realised that nothing could stop me from pursuing further studies. I applied for a scholarship to do a Master of Engineering Science by research and due to my excellent academic achievement I got it.

Minh Hiền's educational journey, The Examiner, July 1987.

While studying for a Master's degree, I also studied English at Rosny College in the evening. I met Farshid there.

A year later we got engaged. We married after my graduation.

*Minh Hiền and Farshid at her Master of Engineering Science graduation,
The University of Tasmania, 1990.*

When I was about to complete a Master of Engineering Science, I got a job with the University of Tasmania in the Faculty of Medicine, located at the Hobart Royal Hospital.

I assisted Dr Michael Lucas to develop a medical application, which we built with a medical doctor, a nurse and a computer programmer, to show on the computer screen a map that represented the electronic signals generated from people's hearts. Doctors would look at the pictures on the computer to assess the current strength of someone's heart and to look for any warning signs. The aim was to assist doctors to diagnose any potential heart diseases early.

Three decades later when I was treated for cancer in Sydney, a nurse would use one of these machines to monitor my heart. I loved that kind of research work.

However, at that time, after Dr Lucas and I built the prototype, the doctor who was in charge of the project could not get the funds needed to commercialise the project.

I did not have an IT degree, but I had studied one IT subject as part of my engineering degree, so I applied for an IT help desk position with the Australian Newsprint Mills (ANM). When a senior engineer, John Ballard, at ANM saw my resume, he immediately called me for an interview. When I arrived at his office, he asked me if I wanted to work as an IT programmer to assist him with computing and engineering matters. When I said yes, he immediately sent me to do a health check.

The Vietnamese Australians: Heritage and Contributions by Minh Hiền

A STORY OF ACHIEVEMENT

AUSTRALIAN Newsprint Mills takes a strong interest in promoting tertiary education in our High School students.

In particular we have put considerable effort into lifting the profile of science education in Tasmania.

Often our commitment to this effort involves practical support or financial assistance to students.

One support exercise we conducted recently was to introduce a number of our graduate staff members to science students in Tasmania.

The story of one staff member in particular is a staggering achievement in not only academic excellence but also in courage and persistance.

With the permission of Hien Tran, a computer programmer attached to Computer Services at Boyer, we have reprinted her story.

Hien beats all the odds

I CAME to Hobart in July 1981 as a refugee from Vietnam. After spending six months learning English and a year studying matriculation at Hobart College, I decided to study Eluctrical Engineering at the University of Tasmania.

In December 1986 I graduated with Honours. I was the only woman graduate electrical engineer at the university that year. For many personal reasons I decided to stay in Tasmania at least for a few more years. Therefore I had to look for a career. Through the University campus I had interviews with many Tasmanian industries but had no luck finding a job. During interviews people commented that they admired my excellent academic results, my ability for hard work and my bravery. As all my year group was employed, I started to think that perhaps practical electrical engineering was only for men. I decided to go into a research field. I went on and studied full-time for my Masters Degree in Control Engineering for 18 months. In October 1988 I applied and gained a job with the University of Tasmania working as a Graduate Research Assistant under a one year contract.

I worked in the Medicine Department designing and developing an x-ray and digital signal processor and computer software to build a data acquisition system that can be used in medical diagnosis.

This one year of work was very helpful to me. It gave me a lot of experience in electronics and computers and I gained a lot of confidence. Also during this period I was undertaking part-time study for my Masters.

I finished the contract with the University in September 1989 and once again it wasn't easy for me to find a job in the research field because in Hobart there isnt much call for research work.

I then decided to go into the computer field as I have enjoyed this field for many years. I applied for a job at Australian Newsprint Mills and I have been employed by ANM as a Computer Programmer since October 1989. I'm enjoying my work and I'm very happy at the moment with my career. My advice to young graduates is that you should analyse your ability and interests and do not just look for a job in only one limited field. You'll find that your knowledge can be used and applied in many other wonderful careers.

Footnote: Hiens story of achievement had another sequel, during April when she attended a graduation ceremony at the University of Tasmania to accept her Masters Degree in Electrical Engineering.

* Hien Tran. . .Analyse your ability and interests.

Minh Hiền's Story of Achivement, the Newsprint Log, 1990.

I loved this job and my supervisor John was very good to me. But I did not like driving two hours every day on the road that was full of trucks. Eighteen months later I resigned. I then worked for an insurance company writing programs to solve money matters. I took the initiative to study accounting to better understand the needs of the company and its customers. My supervisor, Brian Caddell, was so impressed with my work performance that when I said to him that I wanted to leave for another job and wished to have a written reference from him. Brian wrote: "Future employers will profitably and quickly discover her high intellect, absolute reliability, thorough trustworthiness, and her appetite for complex, difficult and important work. Her workmates will also miss the quiet good humour and calmness of the woman. She is respected and well loved. Hien Minh Thi Tran comes with my highest recommendation."

I worked as an Account Information Systems Analyst at the Hydro Electric Commission in Tasmania, which I loved. I developed a new system that generated sales reports for large industries and I converted the old and intensely laborious billing processes to the automated processes which resulted in considerable savings for the Hydro.

However, two years later the Hydro went through a restructure and I was told that my position and my supervisor's position were redundant. My supervisor, Simon Holtby, wrote me a reference before he left the Hydro saying that: "I have absolutely no hesitation in recommending Hien for any appropriate position that requires high levels of commitment to working on complex information system issues."

While working at the Hydro, I used to prepare quarterly reports of power consumption and the revenue earned from major industries in Tasmania for the board members.

When I was delivering the report to the Chief Operations Officer, Ted Pritchard, the second man in charge of the Hydro, I asked if I could see him sometime that afternoon. He readily accepted.

I showed Mr Pritchard a sample of the work which I initiated and completed.

Mr Pritchard said, 'My boys told me that you are overqualified.'

I would never forget those words. I was a young graduate with a Master's degree in engineering and yet the largest engineering company in Tasmania did not have any job for me because Mr Pritchard's boys thought that I was overqualified.

Mr Pritchard's comments did not deter me from adding more qualifications to my profile. Knowing that Sydney is a global city and Australia's main financial and economic centre, I studied for a Master of Commerce for one year which would normally take one-and-a-half years to complete. Then, Farshid and I left Hobart for Sydney.

Minh Hiền at her Master of Commerce graduation
Farshid at his IT Post-graduate graduation, Sydney, 1998.

The Vietnamese Australians: Heritage and Contributions by Minh Hiền

Armed with a Master of Engineering Science and a Master of Commerce, I obtained an excellent job within two weeks of arrival in Sydney.

I was hired as a Systems Design and Project Analyst after I attended two interviews, completed a three-hour test of personality and skills in reasoning, mathematics and English proficiency, and after the new employer conducted reference checking.

I loved that job because I could apply both my engineering and accounting knowledge that I had spent a decade learning and I enjoyed the company of the people I worked with. I got promoted to a managerial role within a year and I received a bonus for my extraordinary contribution to the company. Within two years with the company I was promoted to be in charge of the company's Financial Information Management Systems and supervised four professional staff. It was a private company in the banking industry, yet it had a caring culture.

I loved my job and the people with whom I worked. My direct manager, Angelo Koulos, and his manager, Paul, appreciated my contributions to the company. They showed great respect for education. They sponsored me to complete a Certified Practising Accountant, CPA, and a post-graduate course in Management. I felt I received great rewards for my years of studies.

During that period, we sponsored three children from India through World Vision Australia. The following month, we added another child in Thailand, then another in Cambodia. A few months later, we added eight more Vietnamese children. We sponsored thirteen children through World Vision Australia, donating tens of thousands of dollars. Unfortunately, nine years later, in 2007, when we visited the children in Việt Nam to directly give them some presents from Australia, we stopped donating because we saw our money was mismanaged. Soon after that we read news about World Vision Australia corruption allegations over many years in many countries.

About five years later the organisation where I worked changed drastically. A new CEO, a new Chief of Information and Technology (CIT) were appointed, and the CFO Paul, who hired me, was removed from the company.

A few months later, Angelo left the company. I asked him for a written reference and he wrote: "Hien has exemplified herself as a professional and intuitive individual, who has added enormous value to the Finance Team, and the organisation generally. Her

The Vietnamese Australians: Heritage and Contributions by Minh Hiền

knowledge and expertise has been reflected in the quality and accuracy of her work and management skills - valuable traits to any future role she would fill. With a swag of qualifications including two Bachelors and Masters degrees in Commerce and Engineering; a Graduate Diploma in Management, together with being CPA qualified - she is truly unmatched! She is a committed, honest and hard-working individual, and she has led and mentored her Team of four staff through many pressing deadlines and complex projects, all to great success."

I was young and naive. I thought I would continue working happily at the company. I did not know that the newly appointed CFO, Tom, was planning to remove the former CFO's key employees. Tom hired an external contractor, named Thomas, and gave him full authority to extract information from me. I wrote to the HR department complaining about why I was not given an opportunity to apply for a job that Tom offered to Thomas.

At that time Farshid was working on the North Shore of Sydney. I was working near Sydney's Town Hall, in the middle of the city. We were living in the inner west suburb of Sydney. Farshid almost always stopped at my workplace after work.

Not long after Thomas was hired, Tom bought a large fridge and put it in the room opposite my desk. He stocked it with soft and alcoholic drinks. Every Friday afternoon from 4:00 pm onwards everyone in Finance was allowed to drink at work. Some days Tom brought wine bottles from his own vineyard. I attended the Friday gathering once out of politeness. I ate a small piece of cake then quickly left.

One evening, I was working late. While I was concentrating on running a report on my computer, I smelt alcohol and heard footsteps approaching.

I looked up and saw Thomas, a muscular man with an angry face.

He stopped at my desk and said in a demanding voice, 'Follow me!'

'No,' I said.

'I am waiting for my *husband*.' I emphasised the word husband, hoping that he would leave me alone.

'I have a question for you,' he said.

I saw his face was red.

'You can ask me here,' I spoke rapidly. 'You have any question, you ask me here.'

'Come with me to my room,' he yelled.

'No. I am not going to your room.'

He stared at me.

I was frightened of looking into his bloodshot eyes. I looked down at the keyboard.

From the corner of my eye I saw he picked up the stapler.

As his hand moved upwards, I bent my head down and lifted my hands to shield my eyes.

The metal part of the stapler brushed my hair as it flew past.

A loud bang echoed across the office.

My whole body was shaking.

I looked up. He was disappearing.

The following day, I consulted my GP. She advised me to take time off work and she gave me a medical certificate. When I sent my medical certificate to Jenny, a payroll manager, she said that I should not use my sick leave.

Jenny filled a worker's compensation claim for me and the company admitted liability. The Work Cover appointed an external psychologist to assist me to return to work. She taught me techniques on how to deal with workplace violence and pressured the company to not extend Thomas' contract.

However, not long after my return to work, Tom used the tactics of restructuring the organisation to terminate my employment.

The day after Tom declared my position was redundant I came to the office with a big bag. When I sat down at my desk, I saw that the drawers were open and I noticed that some of the things were missing. My hands were shaking when I picked up a piece of paper on my desk that showed a new organisation chart. I walked fast towards the HR team area. I held the paper in my hand forward towards the HR man who sat at the entrance of the HR team's cubicles.

I said in a determined voice, 'Can I have the position descriptions for all these newly created positions please?'

A young man stood up and asked which position descriptions.

I pointed to the two newly created positions on the new organisation chart. I had qualifications and experiences for both positions.

'I wish to apply for these two positions.' I said firmly.

'Oh!' the HR man murmured, 'We do not have position descriptions for those.'

'So, there is no position description for any of the new positions and yet I have been declared redundant.' I spoke loud and clear.

He asked me to go back to my desk and wait as he needed to check with the CFO.

Fifteen minutes later, he came to me and said that I must go home because I was on garden leave. The expression garden leave was new to me.

I replied to him that 'I have never applied for garden leave. I do not do anything in my garden to take garden leave.'

Garden leave was the leave that big commercial enterprise paid an executive or highly specialised employee to stay at home when they terminated their contractual agreements or made them redundant. It is a euphemism for the company not wanting the person around when they forced them to leave.

The reality was that there were no position descriptions for any of the newly created positions, because the whole re-structuring exercise was just a plan to remove me and another colleague, Mark, whom the new CFO, Tom, did not like because we were both

The Vietnamese Australians: Heritage and Contributions by Minh Hiền

recruited by the former CFO. Mark and I held the two key roles in the finance department. We used to report to a former Group Financial Controller who in turn reported to the previous CFO.

The new CFO Tom wanted to bring his own people to work for him in the key roles.

Tom and the HR department did not expect me to come back to the office to ask for the position descriptions of the new positions to apply because normally when people were made redundant they felt either sad or angry and would call in sick.

Tom could abuse his management power to make me redundant from a permanent job.

But no one could stop me from gaining new knowledge.

I enrolled for a Master of Arts in Creative Writing in order to improve my writing skills.

I loved this course because the writing exercises and assignments kept my mind away from the troubled corporate working life.

Three years later, I completed my third Master's degree.

More importantly I completed my first book, *My Heritage: Vietnam fatherland motherland*, which I launched a few years later.

In September 2007, I started working as a Systems Accountant at a university in Sydney. I settled into my new job quickly.

I enjoyed the quietness of the early hours when I arrived at the university. During lunch break, I would often sit near the entry of the library and would see students queuing for a computer. The atmosphere of the library at this university reminded me of my early years at the University of Tasmania. Sitting in the library, as I watched students walking in and out of the library, I remembered with joy my own student life decades earlier.

I had no problem with returning to work after a long break.

I enjoyed working and going to the university because I had always thought highly of education.

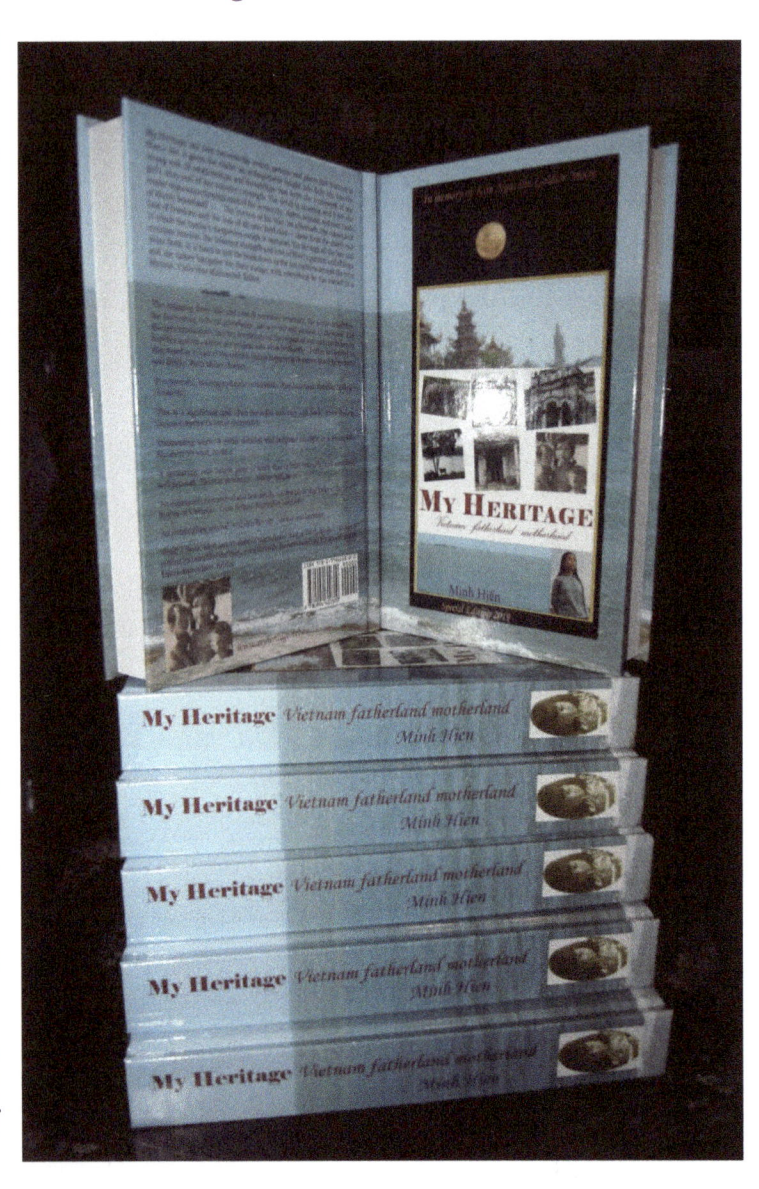

The Vietnamese Australians: Heritage and Contributions by Minh Hiền

When we stopped our donations to the World Vision Australia, we sent money to the University of Tasmania to support refugee students and to Việt Nam to support poor children in schools. We regularly visited my ancestral village in Việt Nam to give scholarships to the students directly ourselves.

Minh Hiền and Farshid provided scholarships to village students.

While working at the university, I taught undergraduate students as well as staff and managers every year for almost ten years. I also provided consultancy and advanced training to specialists such as Revenue Officers, Account Payable Officers, Purchasing Officers, Budgeting Officers, Finance Coordinators, Finance Officers, Accountants, Auditors and Finance Managers.

I knew the university's financial systems in depth and I had a great passion for teaching. I often went well beyond my duties to make sure finance users understood the financial systems and could perform their duties. When I was asked to prepare User Training Manuals and deliver training to 250 finance users on the General Ledger Chart Restructure, I spent my personal time to ensure that the training manuals were ready in time for training. I trained all 250 finance users within three weeks. My training workshops were attended by a wide range of professional staff such as Faculty General Managers, Finance Managers, Auditors, Accountants, Executive Assistants to Deans as well as academic staff such as Professors, Post-graduate Students and Researchers.

I prepared very detailed documents as well as summary materials to suit the diverse group of users of the systems. I conducted training workshops every fortnight and held regular finance clinics. My workshops and clinics were very popular. I received copious praise for the quality of my training from staff, Directors, Faculty General Managers, Accountants, Department Manager and Administration Officers. Over the years, I wrote eight volumes of training documents for finance users, between 100 and 350 pages each volume. Many staff would print my training manuals in colour, bind them and keep them for reference.

In 2007, when I joined the university I had already completed a Master of Arts in Writing, a Master of Commerce, a Master of Engineering Science, a Graduate Diploma in Management, a Graduate Conversion Course in Accounting, a Bachelor of Engineering with honours and a CPA. While working at the university, I initiated and conducted my own research and received the *Foundations in Learning and Teaching Alumni Runner-Up Scholarship*.

Minh Hiền with Dr Marina Harvey, Sydney, 2014.

I also studied for a Master of Higher Education which I completed in 2016 with Distinctions and received a Certificate of Achievement from the School of Education. Prior to that, I had studied a few subjects of a Diploma in Law. However, I chose to complete the Master of Higher Education over the Diploma in Law because I wanted to gain an understanding of higher education and to teach university students better.

The Vietnamese Australians: Heritage and Contributions by Minh Hiền

I regularly took annual leave and self-funded for my overseas trips to speak about my teaching experiences at international conferences held in Europe, Asia and Canada. During my personal time I conducted research on how adults learn. The topics of my research were the effects of personality on learning and how best to design course materials to teach people with different personality traits and knowledge. I studied in the evenings. I studied on the bus while travelling to work. I conducted research and wrote papers during weekends. I presented IT and education papers at conferences on Information Systems Management and Evaluation and conferences on Computer Research and Development. I also published papers in various international journals. I received the 2017 *Best Paper Award* for the European Alliance for Innovation (EAI) International Conference on Nature of Computation and Communication for my research work on the design of online learning resources to teach university staff accounting information.

Minh Hiền and Farshid at the IT and Education conference, Sài Gòn, 2013.

Minh Hiền at the IT and Education conference in Nha Trang, Việt Nam, 2015.

The Vietnamese Australians: Heritage and Contributions by Minh Hiền

Minh Hiền travelled to Europe to present her papers at the IT and Accounting conference, 2014.

After working at the university for ten years, Farshid and I travelled to the Quảng Nam University in Tam Kỳ, Việt Nam to present our papers about online teaching at the IT conference.

Minh Hiền and Farshid at the Quảng Nam University, Việt Nam, 2017.

While we were in Tam Kỳ there was a flood that stopped us from going to Huế which was our next destination, so we stayed in Tam Kỳ for ten more days to teach English to students at the Quảng Nam University and to children at private English classes, operating from home by English teachers, Diệu Hiền and Kiều Ngân. We observed that Vietnamese parents worked very hard to send their children to private English classes.

The Vietnamese Australians: Heritage and Contributions by Minh Hiền

Minh Hiền with students in Kiều Ngân's English classes, Tam Kỳ, Việt Nam, 2017.

Minh Hiền teaching at the Quảng Nam University in Tam Kỳ, Việt Nam, 2017.

A few weeks later we delivered an online teaching course from Australia to the second-year students and Farshid conducted surveys for his PhD project. Our teaching was purely voluntary. Six months later we gave a speech about our teaching at the *Language, Society and Culture* conference in Huế, Việt Nam.

Minh Hiền and Farshid at the Language & Culture conference in Huế, Việt Nam, 2018.

The Vietnamese Australians: Heritage and Contributions by Minh Hiền

A few weeks later, I was diagnosed with breast cancer. While the chemo drugs were dripping drop-by-drop into my veins, I saw on Facebook that the whole town where my students were studying was under water. The water had risen so high that none of my students could go to university. I posted messages to encourage my students to spend time studying online with me while they were disconnected from their normal classes. I posted activities for them to study. I encouraged them to learn English in teams and to support each other during times of difficulty. I read and commented on their posts.

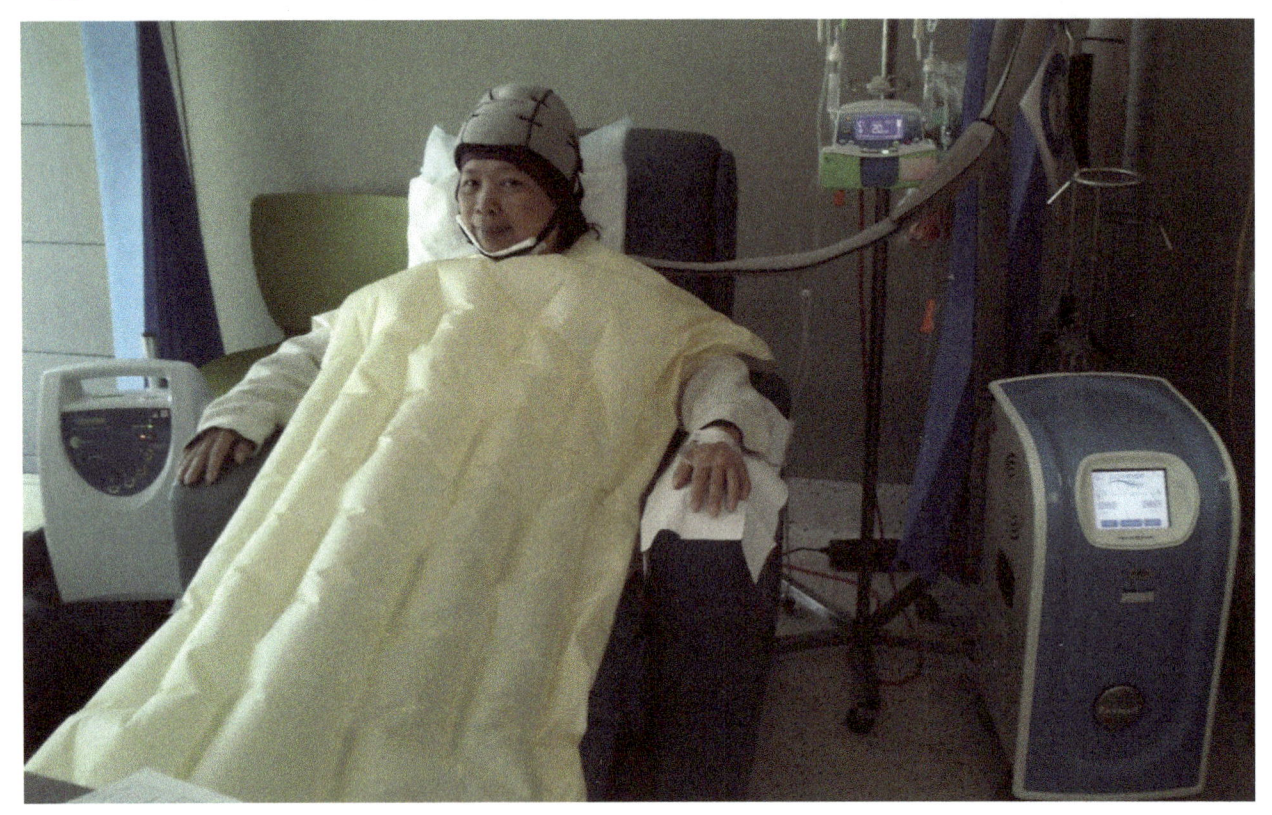

Minh Hiền, Sydney, 2018.

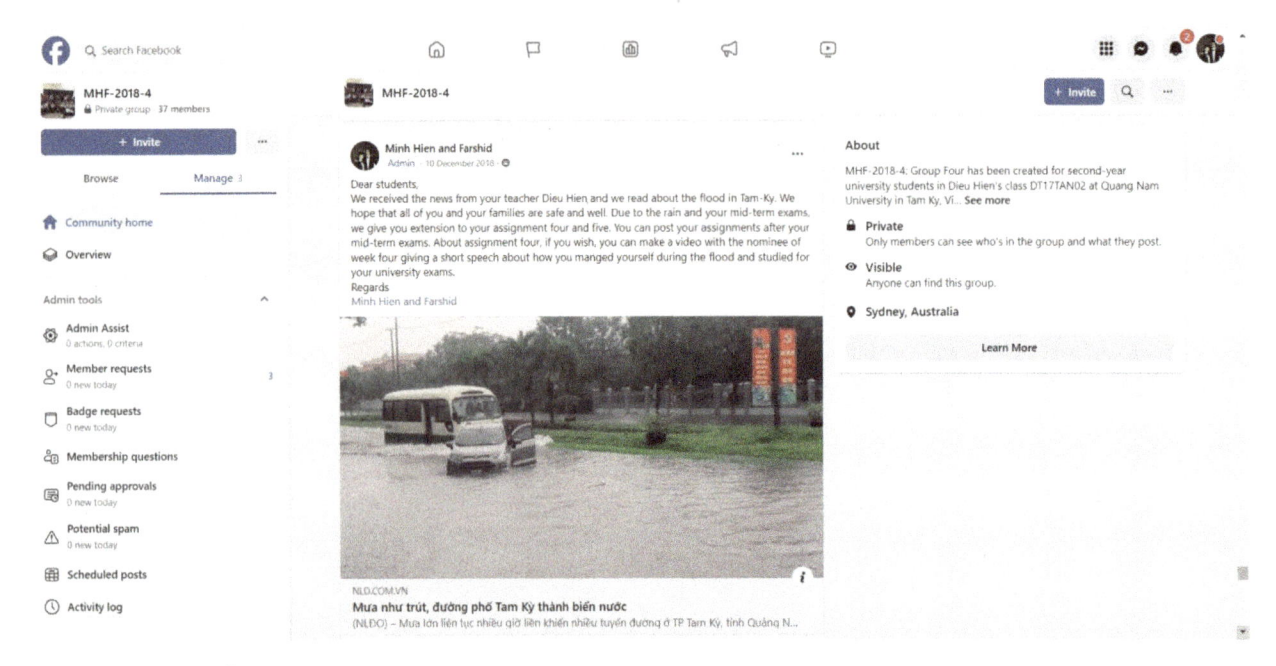

Minh Hiền's messages to her online students during the 2018 flood in Tam Kỳ.

The Vietnamese Australians: Heritage and Contributions by Minh Hiền

When my hair started to grow back, Farshid and I travelled to Việt Nam to meet our students and to take my online students to the Viet TESOL conference in Huế.

Minh Hiền with her students at the Quảng Nam University, Tam Kỳ, Việt Nam, 2019.

Minh Hiền and Farshid with their students and teacher Diệu Hiền at the Viet TESOL conference in Huế, 2019.

Minh Hiền and Farshid celebrated with their students in Huế, October 2019.

While I was under cancer treatment, Farshid was doing a PhD in computing.

In May 2019, we travelled to Canada to present our papers at the premier *International Conference on Software Engineering* (ICSE).

We had written these papers for the ICSE after my second operation for breast cancer and after the news that Farshid's elder brother in Iran had passed away.

At that time, Farshid's mind was not into writing papers for conferences.

Farshid needed someone to talk and to discuss his PhD project.

Hence, I co-authored and co-presented with Farshid many of his PhD papers.

Minh Hiền and Farshid, Montréal, Canada, May 2019.

The Vietnamese Australians: Heritage and Contributions by Minh Hiền

During the Covid-19 lockdown, Farshid and I continued teaching online to students from rural areas of Việt Nam and presented our papers virtually at conferences in Spain and in Việt Nam. We gave scholarships to ten students who completed our online courses.

In August 2023, when the threat of Covid-19 was over, we went to Việt Nam to present our papers at the Viet TESOL conference, to meet our students and to give scholarships.

Minh Hiền and Farshid at the Viet TESOL conference, Hà Nội, August 2023.

The Vietnamese Australians: Heritage and Contributions by Minh Hiền

Minh Hiền and Farshid with the recipients of their scholarships and teachers at the Quang Nam University - Vinh Linh and Diệu Hiền - Tam Kỳ, September 2023.

Minh Hiền with second-year students, Tam Kỳ, September 2023.

Minh Hiền with third-year students, teacher Diệu Hiền and teacher Ngàn Thương, Tam Kỳ, September 2023.

Minh Hiền and Farshid with final-year students, Tam Thanh Beach, September 2023.

Minh Hiền and Farshid with Thủy Nguyên, a student in Kiều Ngân's English class, Nguyên's younger sister and mother, and Kiều Ngân, Tam Kỳ, 2017.

Minh Hiền and Farshid with Thủy Nguyên and her mother six years later, Tam Thanh Beach, September 2023.

While teaching English to students at the Quảng Nam University, I also studied for a Master of Education at the University of New South Wales online. I wanted to make sure that I had good knowledge of educational studies to teach my students. Through the studies, I had a better understanding of how students learn and their needs and, I developed learning materials for my students accordingly.

I often reflect on Buddha's teaching that: 'Your mind is a powerful thing. When you filter it with positive thoughts, your life will start to change.'

I am a former refugee from a non-English speaking country and a survivor of breast cancer. When I came to Australia without my parents and at the age of eighteen, I had no knowledge of the English language. Since then, I have completed eight university qualifications in the fields of Engineering, Accounting, Commerce, Management, Arts, and Education and a qualification as a professional member of the Australian Society of CPA. I have worked in various professions and I have taught thousands of people. While working at university, I received more than 500 pages of positive feedback from managers and staff through the online surveys that I conducted regularly.

Minh Hiền and Farshid at the river in front of their Sydney home, October 2023.

I passionately believe in education as having the power to transform people's lives.

I have devoted my life to education and through education my husband and I have achieved financial independence and have our own homes. I feel that I am the product of the excellent education system that Australia can offer. I want to help disadvantaged people through the power of education by teaching them what I know. I hope that my stories will inspire others, especially the socially and economically disadvantaged youths, to advance their life conditions through education.

The Spirit of Vietnamese Martial Arts

My eldest brother, Tri, has loved martial arts since childhood. He was trained by some of the very best martial arts teachers in Sâi Gòn since he was a child. By the time Tri arrived in Australia, he had a senior / experienced black-belt.

Tri was handsome, cheerful, well built, strong and skilled in martial arts. He was outgoing and could make friends easily. He practised martial arts in the gym at the University of Tasmania a few days a week. Some young Australians approached him and asked him to teach them.

Tri hired a gym at the University of Tasmania three nights a week and a few hours during the weekends to practise and to teach Vietnamese Martial Arts, *Việt Võ*. Tri never collected any payment from his students other than a small membership fee to contribute to the cost of hiring the gym and to buy equipment for training.

When Tri first arrived in Australia as a refugee, he found Australia a very kind country; he wanted to somehow repay its kindness.

Australian friends told him: 'Not to worry about it because in Australia you will have to pay tax for the rest of your life.'

'Well,' Tri said, 'you are right but everyone does that.'

Tri decided to contribute his unique skills for free to Australia.

Tri Tri Tran, Training in a park, Hobart, 1981.

In August 1980, Tri's Việt Võ club commenced with seven or eight people. The treasurer and the secretary collected money weekly or monthly to pay for the bills. The treasurer kept the fund and the secretary kept the record of payments. They decided how to spend the money. They only asked Tri what equipment to buy for the club. Tri never allocated any money to himself.

When Tri arrived in Sydney in the mid-1990s, an old admirer had just opened a large gym in the city, he offered Tri a very good salary to teach part time at his gym. Tri politely refused. Sometime later Tri taught for free at a non-profit organisation in Fairfield as he wished to contribute to the Australian community for its kindness.

Tri Tri Tran, Training at the University of Tasmania gym, 1980.

Tri was the first Vietnamese Australian to hold the title of the *Australian Open Kung-Fu Championship*. The Australian Open Kung-Fu Championship is different from the Australian Championship. *Open* means all styles participate as opposed to different styles have different Australian championships and only its members are allowed to participate, such as Taekwondo, Judo and most Karate styles.

Tri held the *Australian Open Kung-Fu Championship* for the record of seven consecutive years. He also won the *Kick Boxing Championship* three times during those years. Many martial arts people, especially among the Vietnamese communities in Tasmania, Victoria, NSW and QLD, hold Tri in high regard. Overseas martial arts teachers from the USA, Canada, the Philippines and Việt Nam often sought him out and met him when they visited Australia.

Tri Tri Tran, Sydney Town Hall, 1984.

In Tasmania, every martial artist spoke highly of my three brothers.

My second elder-brother, Trí Tuệ, who was the tallest one in our family and was bigger than an average Vietnamese man, was the senior Việt Võ instructor and a referee for hundreds of States and National Championships matches. He was also the manager for

The Vietnamese Australians: Heritage And Contributions by Minh Hiền

the Việt Võ team when they competed at the State and the National competitions. Like Tri, Tuệ was also outgoing and could make friends easily.

Trí Tuệ (Tri Tue Tran) and Trí Tri (Tri Tri Tran), Sydney, 1984.

The photo was taken at the home of Trí Tri's new friend, Master Hung Ly, who watched the Championship and was so impressed that he invited Tri and Tuệ to his home.

Master Hung Ly was a Shaolin teacher and a Feng Shui expert who is now 'Seven Dan' in Shaolin, teaching at the *Dong Tam Association* for the last thirty years plus. He is also a Feng Shui Master who has written hundreds of articles in many newspapers and magazines in Australia and the US about Martial Arts and Feng Shui and a book on Feng Shui.

Martial artists called my youngest brother *Bear*.

This name started from members of Tri's Việt Võ club.

They called him *Bear* instead of Bé.

Bé's nickname was given to him by Tri because Tri was six years older than Bé, so he used to carry Bé on his back when Bé was small.

In our family, we called my youngest brother Bé.

Tri also called him Bé in his Việt Võ club. However, the people at Tri's club called Bé Bear because he fought like a bear on two legs, which is not pretty or elegant like other top fighters of his club but very scary and effective.

In August 1989, when Bé fought in Melbourne there was a group of teenagers, wearing Teddy Bear T-shirts and some even carried Teddy Bears to form the Bear's fan group.

Bé won six State Championships and the Australian and South Pacific Championship.

He also was voted number one of the twenty top athletes of Tasmania in its Inaugural annual ceremony and he received a statue similar to an Oscar.

Tri Minh Tran (Bé) was using Peter, the manager of Mount Saint Canice Migrant Hostel where most refugees stayed when first arrived, as a 'target practice'. Peter was a very keen Việt Võ practitioner. The University of Tasmania Oval, Sandy Bay, 1983.

I went with my three brothers sometimes to watch their training sessions, their fighting in the competitions and their annual grading.

I would often watch Tri teach his students to practise mindfulness at every opportunity.

I could see there was a deep bond among members of Tri's Việt Võ club.

Othma Buchmann, Tri Tri Tran, Pat Scanlon
Training at the University of Tasmania gym, 1980

Othma Buchmann was a lecturer at the University of Tasmania. He held a Third Dan Karate at the time. He is Tri's good friend. Sensei Othma retired at seventh Dan a few years ago.

Pat Scanlon was one of Tri's very first Việt Võ students. Twelve months later Pat left Tasmania to teach English in Japan, where he obtained his black-belt in Karate within two months of training. Sensei Pat also retired a few years ago when he was at fifth Dan.

Tri Minh Tran (Bé) (most right) with Rachael Robins (and her daughter Christie), Mark (far left) and Robert Oakley (sitting) at the informal weekend class, The University of Tasmania gym, 1983.

Rachael Robins ran a model agency and school. She is retired.

Mark later became an Associate Professor of Law.

Robert Oakley was the 'best looking' mechanic at the time and a fearsome fighter. He won the *Inaugural Tasmanian Middle-Weight* title. Robert was a proud *Việt Võ* member. He insisted on having the Việt Võ logo hand-embroidered on his martial arts uniform but he could not find anyone who could do it. Tuệ asked me to help. In 2008, Robert donated his *Tasmanian martial arts uniforms* to the *Tasmanian Museum and Art Gallery* under the *Cultural Heritage*[8].

Tri told me the Vietnamese Martial Arts, Việt Võ, were not just about kicking and punching; the spirit of Vietnamese Martial Arts is to learn to strengthen the mind, the spirit and the body.

Many of Tri's students understood that.

In 2014, Steve Mars, who was Tri's student and also a teacher of Việt Võ, posted on Facebook:

"for those that may be thinking about starting out on the Viet Vo path…let me just say quite seriously Viet Vo effectively saved my life…after a major stroke in 2000 it was Tri and what I had learnt in the previous 20 years that allowed me to walk again and use my right arm and hand again… all of which was supposed to be impossible… if you put in the time and effort Viet Vo can offer you just so much…and enjoy a few beers with the troops along the way…go for it."

Steve had retired from teaching Việt Võ for a year or two before he had a stroke.

After Steve's remarkably recovery from his stroke, he was awarded another stripe/degree on his Back belt.

A senior black-belt holder asked Tri: 'I'm not jealous with Steve or anything like that I just want to know how our senior award/grading system works.'

Tri replied, 'If you win the World Championship you will be awarded another degree just like Steve.'

'Yes,' said the senior black-belt holder. 'I understand about being awarded for achievement at the highest level and bringing honour to our school but…'

'No but,' Tri stopped him. 'What Steve's done and achieved is far more important, more significant than winning the World title.'

The senior black-belt holder was bewildered but kept quiet.

Many years later, he told his students in a speech that was one of the best lessons he had learned from Việt Võ.

Tri Tri Tran and Steve Mars at the University of Tasmania gym, 1986.

Việt Võ has deep spiritual connections with the Vietnamese culture and history.

Việt Võ was born out of necessity to protect the Vietnamese from foreign invaders since ancient times. It had advanced to the same status as literature in the national school system during the time of General Trần Hưng Đạo who was made a Saint by the Vietnamese.

After winning the first bloody battle against the Mongolian invaders, the Vietnamese Emperor Trần Nhân Tông and General Trần Hưng Đạo knew that the Mongolian army would return for revenge and to fulfil their ambitions.

To prepare for this, they gathered Martial Arts masters throughout Việt Nam to enlist their aid.

This was the turning point in the history of the Vietnamese Martial Arts as it was the first time that Martial Arts masters from different schools worked together for a common and noble cause.

The Mongol army could move with incredible speed and their soldiers were extremely skilful on horse-back with their bows and arrows. The Vietnamese Martial Arts masters agreed that the best tactic would be to separate the Mongolian soldiers from their horses. The question was how.

Legend has it that after weeks of studying horses' habits and exchanging techniques, the Martial Arts assembly developed a new technique that involved using shields to protect the Vietnamese soldier from arrows and to avoid being crushed by the horses' hooves while using broadswords to attack the horses' legs and then they taught sturdily built soldiers the new technique.

In addition to the *broad-swords and shields rolling* technique, another interesting technique developed during this time for "foot-soldiers" to use against the cavalry was the *flying or leaping kick* technique, since the movement of a man on horse-back is quite slow and awkward.

When Mongol Prince Toghan led an army and seized the capital of Việt Nam, Thăng Long - now Hà Nội, in the surrounding provinces soldiers who had been trained how to use broad-swords and shields, rolled under the horses' hooves and attacked the horses' legs; they managed to separate the Mongol soldiers from their horses. Meanwhile Emperor Trần Nhân Tông escorted by General Trần Hưng Đạo withdrew from the capital.

Soldiers put up posters to encourage people to resist the invaders by all means and, if necessary, to take refuge in the jungles and mountains. After burning off most of their crops and facilities, all Vietnamese retreated.

When the Mongol army had been worn down with tropical diseases and lack of supplies, Trần Hưng Đạo launched a counter-offensive on the waterfronts where the Mongols could not use their cavalry strength. Mongol commander Sogetu of the Southern front was killed in the battle. In their withdrawal from Việt Nam, the Mongols were also attacked by the Hmong and Yao minorities in the Northern regions.

The Vietnamese Australians: Heritage and Contributions by Minh Hiền

Trần Hưng Đạo had written *Binh Thư Yếu Lược*, a Book on Military Strategies, and *Hịch Tướng Sĩ*, a Proclamation to Generals and Soldiers to inspire them to fight against the Mongol invaders with great success. His writings were used as textbooks for military training. It had lifted the spirit of the generals and soldiers who fought the Mongols as well as the spirit of the Vietnamese Australians.

In September 1984 when Tri fought his opponent who lived in New South Wales, the Vietnamese Australians living in Sydney saw that Tri represented them.

A few weeks before the Championship started, the organisation, the *National Kick Boxing Federation*, advertised in the Vietnamese newspapers a small photo of Tri with a headline of the Championship, the date, time and location.

That small picture of Tri was enough to fire up thousands of Vietnamese Australians in Sydney to queue up to get tickets.

On the day, almost one third of the people in the Sydney Town Hall were Vietnamese Australians. None of them knew Tri. Tasmania had been too far away and too cold for these Vietnamese Australians to visit. They were anxious to have a glimpse of Tri as if he was their long lost brother who had been separated from them because of the long war in Việt Nam.

Credit © The Việt Luận, The Vietnamese Herald, 1984.

Sydney had the largest Vietnamese community in Australia. Almost all Vietnamese had arrived in Australia from one of the refugee camps in South East Asia. When they saw the advertisement in the Vietnamese newspapers, they saw themselves through Tri, who had also arrived in Australia from a refugee camp.

Both my elder brothers, Trí Tri and Trí Tuệ, who flew from Hobart to Sydney on that day, were refugees.

Four months before that, in May 1984, Tri had won the *Australian Open Kung Fu Championship* in Melbourne Town Hall.

Now, Tri came to Sydney Town Hall for his second Championship title. Tuệ was Tri's right-hand man.

When Tri entered the ring, he was greeted by roaring sounds of applause and cheer, followed by the warm and nostalgic sounds, *Việt Nam Chào Mừng*, screaming from the floor by thousands of Vietnamese Australians.

Tri's spirit lifted. He must win.

That year, the Year of the Mouse 1984, Tri won two of the biggest titles in Australia.

Winning two different National Championships within a four-month period was never heard of. This compares with nowadays winning a National Boxing title and a National Open Martial Arts title or a National Wrestling title and a National Judo title at the same time. Because at the top level, whether it is fighting or racing or shooting or archery or fencing or even golf, participants operate through instinct and reflex, honed by thousands of repetitions. Their mind is almost blank, the reflex and instinct take over. Different styles or titles have different rules and techniques, some techniques are allowed and even encouraged in one but they are forbidden in another.

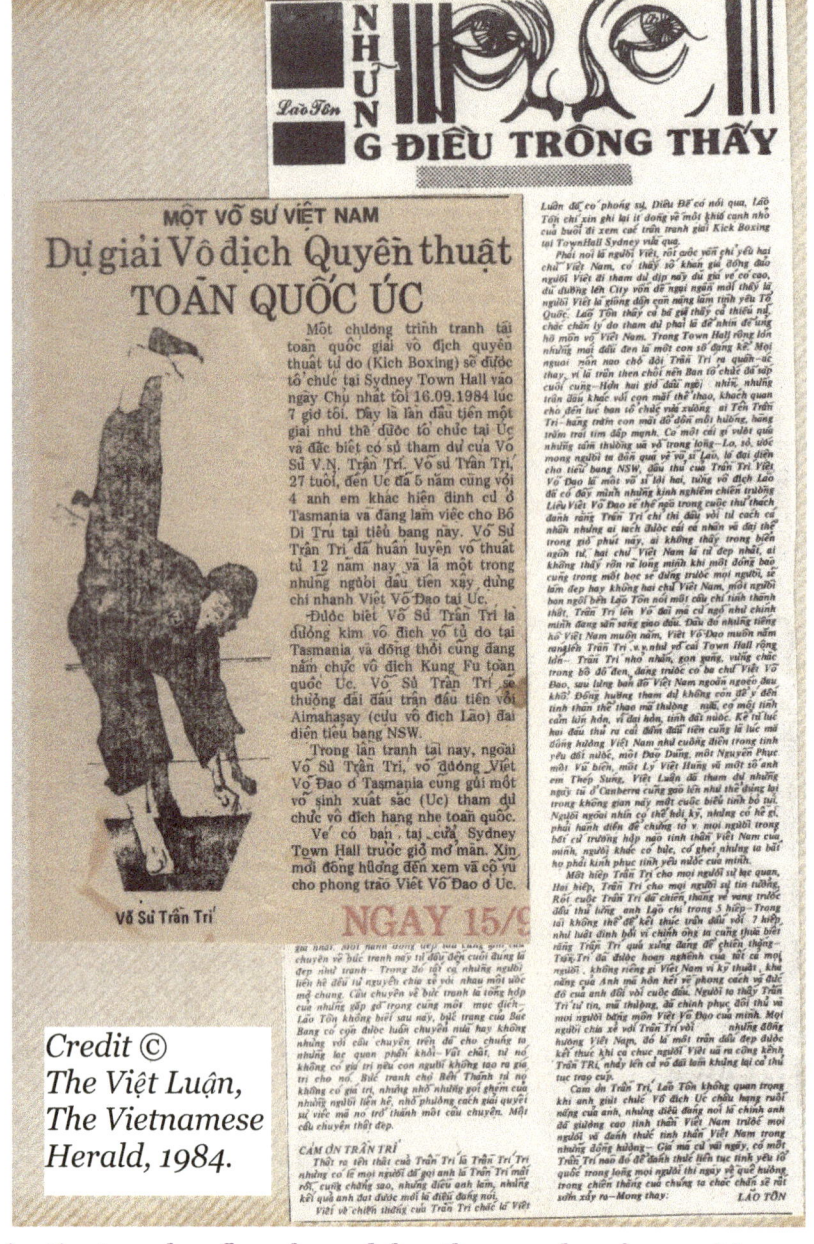

Credit ©
The Việt Luận,
The Vietnamese
Herald, 1984.

Tri's photos and stories appeared on the front pages of all the Vietnamese Community newspapers in Australia and all the major newspapers in Tasmania.

The Vietnamese Australian Communities, especially Vietnamese men in NSW, VIC and TAS, roared with excitement. Four decades later many people still speak of Tri's achievements in Vietnamese Martial Arts. Some have become Tri's friends.

The Philosophy of Vietnamese Martial Arts

Việt Võ is more than a sport because the proper Việt Võ masters train their students to gain strength physically, mentally and emotionally.

For example, Tri taught his students *Mindfulness Martial Arts* at training sessions and when 'having a shower'.

> After training, when you have a shower, you have to be mindful of the soap, shampoo and sensation of water on the skin.
>
> Do not sing in the shower or think of anything else or try to finish it quickly so that you can do something else.
>
> Take your time to enjoy the shower.
>
> And the shower not only washes of the sweat, dirt, grime of the body but also of the mind.
>
> The mantra was,
>
>> 'I'm washing off all dirt from my body and also from my Mind.
>>
>> I wash away all worries, annoyances, anxiety, and fear as well.'
>
> Focus totally on this mantra.
>
> Feel it.
>
> This also applies to when you wash your face or brush your teeth.

Tri did not always give direct instructions about 'washing the mind' to his students.

He often quietly introduced the Việt Võ philosophy to them. For example, Tri told me that in one novice fight i.e. the first or the second time the fighter fights, one of Tri's students was losing badly in the first round. Tri could tell that this student's mind was yelling and shouting inside his head with the wrong dialogue.

Below is what Tri's student said long after that day.

> I was scared. I thought I would shit in my pants.
>
> Suddenly, Tri climbed into the ring. He never got involved with junior fighters.
>
> He just watched and later told you what you did wrong or right.
>
> After allowing me to breathe and wash my mouth and have a sip of water, Tri whispered in my ear, 'Be quiet.'
>
> I was thinking to myself, oh no! Not one of your Vietnamese riddles, which take me two years to understand and in the meantime, I'm toasted.
>
> It looked like Tri could read my mind.
>
> He smiled broadly and said, 'Quiet and Silent your MIND and just DO IT'.
>
> The bell rang, the second round started.

What's he talking about?

What kind of advice is this?

Then, suddenly, I heard and realised what my mind was thinking and saying ... all negative things.

And, I just 'do it'.

The combinations and techniques he made me do a thousand times in the last few months just poured out.

I almost knocked my opponent out cold.

But the decision was a draw.

Most people think I should win outright but I didn't care.

I learned the best lesson in my life.

I never fight again.

Like, I said, I almost shitted in my pants.

But, in my business life, I'm very successful, retire early and very comfortably.

And when I scared shitless, I always remember the words:

'Quiet, Silence your mind,' Tri whispered in my ear many decades ago.

Tri often said the followings to his Black-belt or Degree/Dan Gradings students. These were the seniors as in ranks not in age students.

You have learnt and practiced Việt Võ for many years. How many times did you actually need 'it' to protect or defend for yourself or someone you care?

Most of the time, the answers are 'None'.

Tri said, 'at a different time or different places on earth Việt Võ skills are very valuable, not so in the contemporary Australian society.

We are practicing Việt Võ not to defeat anybody, really, but to defeat ourselves.

Defeat our own Fears, Defeat our own Anger,

Defeat our hatred and Deafening the scary and noisy voice in our heads.

Thus, free ourselves to live a more enjoyable and more peaceful and more fulfilling lives.'

Below is an incident that happened to Tri during his Championship in Sydney in 1984.

Master Hung Ly was so impressed by Tri's response that he invited Tri and Tuệ to his home for dinner and he talked about that incident many times and many decades later.

Tri's opponent was losing badly and started using illegal techniques.

The Vietnamese Australians: Heritage and Contributions by Minh Hiền

The worst one in Martial Arts is kicking your opponent's groin to scare him from lifting his leg up. Kicking the head or the ribs is perfectly legal and encouraged. Kicking the groin is not. It's extreme un-sportsmanship and it is not allowed. This dirty tactic is used to prevent your opponent from attacking and knocking you out and win the fight if the referee doesn't see it.

The first time Tri's opponent used this trick, the American referee warned him.

In the next round, he did it twice. The third time was more powerful and more obvious. The referee stopped the fight and deducted points.

Tri was obviously in pain.

The referee asked Tri, 'Do you want to continue the fight? If you can't, I'll disqualify him and you win. You are a new Australian Champion.'

Tri said, 'No, I don't want to win like that. It was probably an accident. He didn't mean to.'

'This is the third time he has done it,' said the referee.

'He's probably hurt and dazed,' said Tri. 'He might do it unintentionally. Let me finish the fight'.

'Ok,' said the referee, 'it's your call, let's fight'.

Tri knocked his opponent out in the fifth round of the scheduled seven rounds of the Championship. The roar of the crowd was deafening. The Vietnamese Australian spectators invaded the ring and the security guards had a hard time to control the crowd.

Tri had not just won his second *National Championship* within four months. He had brought eminence to the whole Vietnamese Community in Australia.

It was 1984. It was a time when none of us, the Vietnamese Australians, could imagine ever returning to Việt Nam, our fatherland, our motherland, during our life time.

The Vietnamese Martial Arts have very deep roots in our culture and history. For thousands of years our ancestors had to continually develop techniques to fight foreign invaders. Learning martial arts is ingrained in most Vietnamese men and appreciated by most Vietnamese women. In Việt Nam, most mothers and fathers would send their sons to learn martial arts, like here in Australia parents send their children to after school activities.

Almost all Vietnamese Australians had embarked on very difficult and hazardous journeys to Australia. Almost all men and women had lost members of their family or were traumatised whether during the war or during their escape in a small fishing boat. In Australia, they struggled to learn a new culture and a new language while working long hours in factories or bending their head over a Singer sewing machine into wee hours, seven days a week, 365 days a year to make ends meet and better the future of their children.

The Vietnamese Australians were nostalgic and longed to retain their culture and customs in their new homeland. Their sentiments towards Tri's Martial Arts Championship achievements were beyond words. Many approached Tri after that and said that they were proud of him. They admired him for his gentleness and humility. Tuệ told me that the Vietnamese Community leaders and the Vietnamese press literally kidnapped Tri for two days.

Tri delivers a sidekick to his exponent on his way to his national title, 1984.

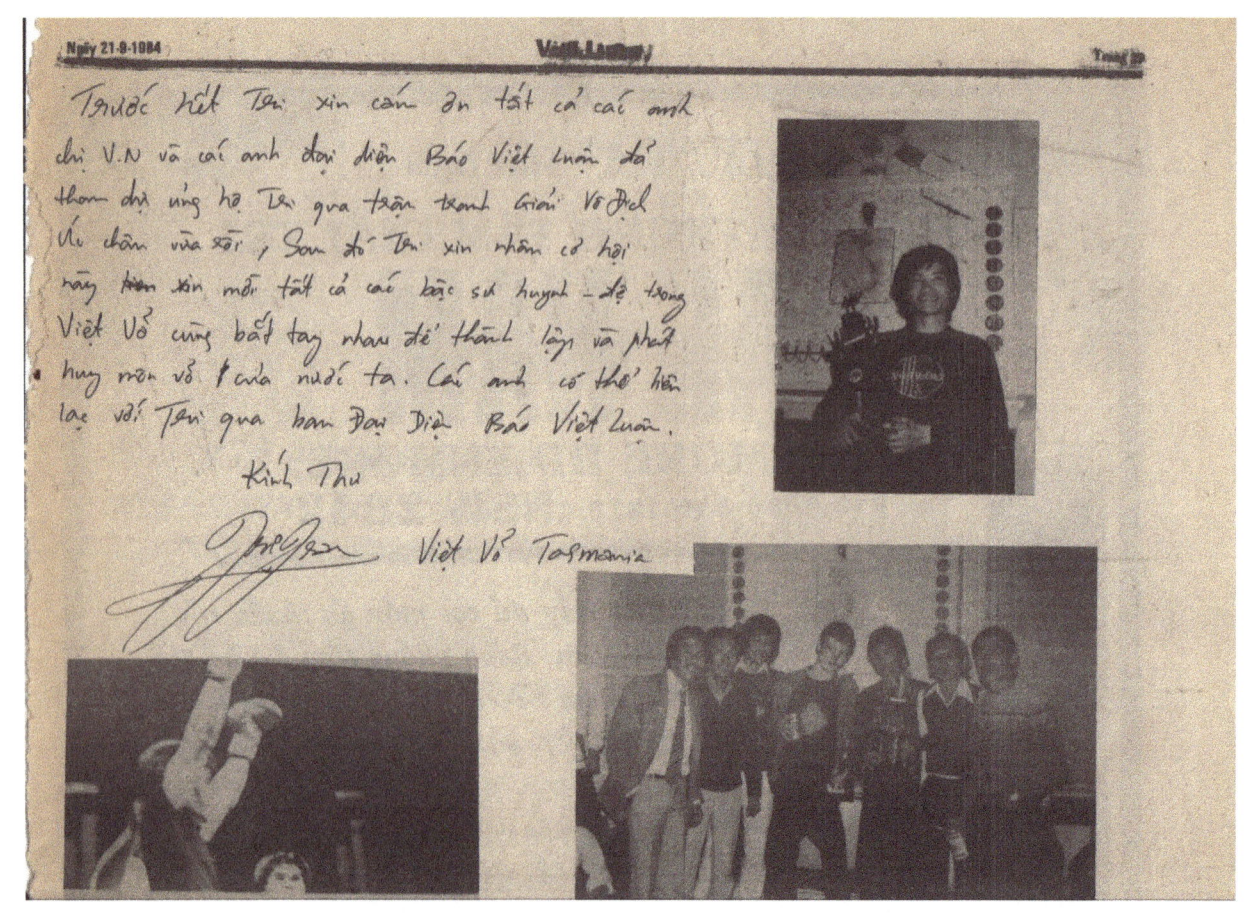

The Việt Luận, The Vietnamese Herald, 1984.

Optimism

'Positive thoughts create positive energy', said my father to us when we were children.

Việt Võ history instils optimism in the learners. Việt Võ teaches learners techniques to successfully fight for independence as well as to build confidence. In Australia, Tri taught his students both physical and mental exercises and relaxation. Tri's students learnt to control their mind and body as well as learn and practice moral values such as respect for others, faithfulness and patience. These lessons built their confidence.

I met many members of Tri's Việt Võ club. They came from all walks of life. They were respectful and supportive of one another. They were optimistic about life.

Tri Tri Tran and his student, Florian Sonner, 1984.

Tri Minh Tran (Bé) and Tri's student, Rachael Robins, University of Tasmania, 1985.

Tri Tri Tran's students, Hobart, during the 1980s.

Tri Tri Tran
The Sunday Tasmanian, 11 August 1985.

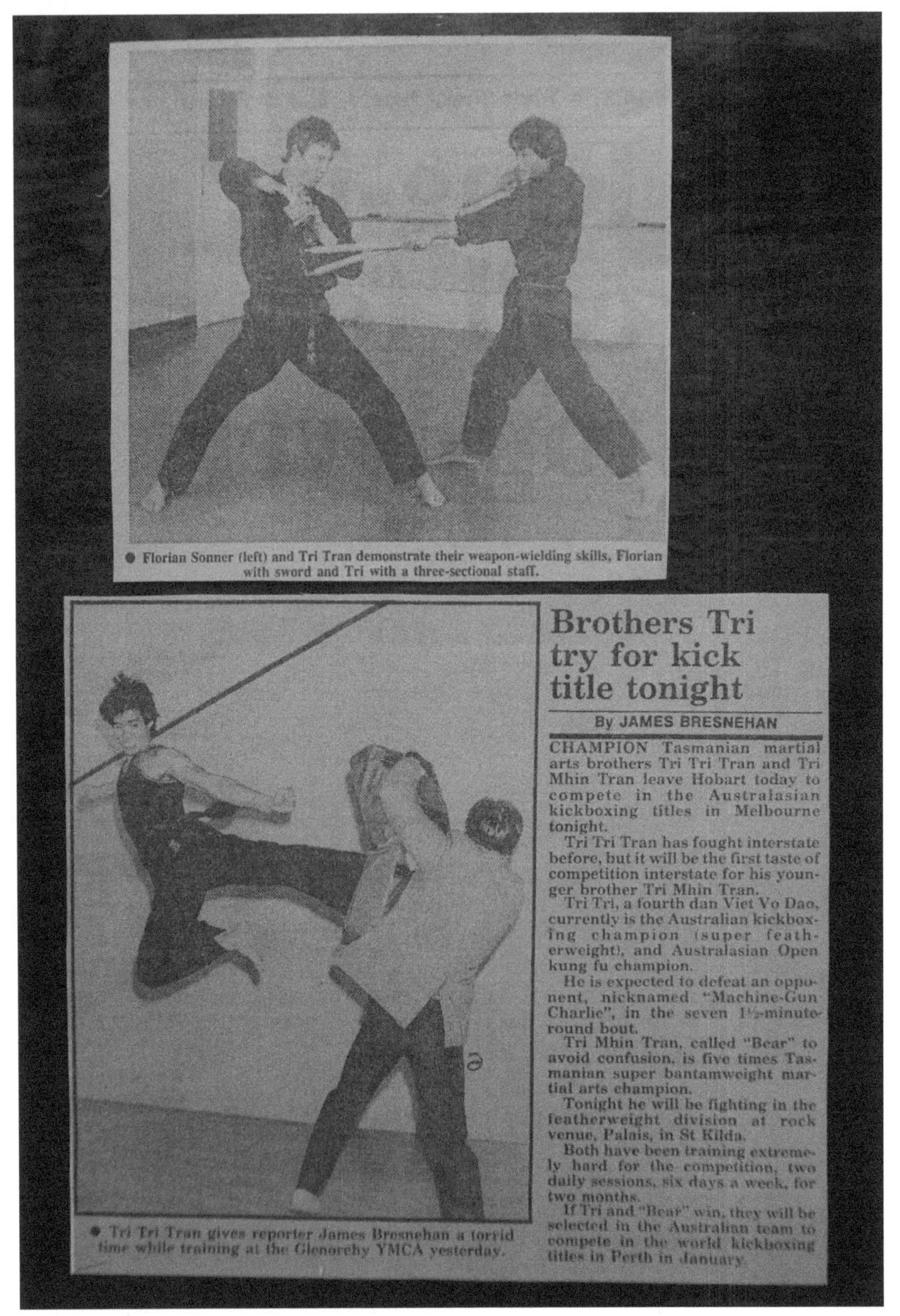

● Florian Sonner (left) and Tri Tran demonstrate their weapon-wielding skills, Florian with sword and Tri with a three-sectional staff.

Brothers Tri try for kick title tonight

By JAMES BRESNEHAN

CHAMPION Tasmanian martial arts brothers Tri Tri Tran and Tri Mhin Tran leave Hobart today to compete in the Australasian kickboxing titles in Melbourne tonight.

Tri Tri Tran has fought interstate before, but it will be the first taste of competition interstate for his younger brother Tri Mhin Tran.

Tri Tri, a fourth dan Viet Vo Dao, currently is the Australian kickboxing champion (super featherweight), and Australasian Open kung fu champion.

He is expected to defeat an opponent, nicknamed "Machine-Gun Charlie", in the seven 1½-minute-round bout.

Tri Mhin Tran, called "Bear" to avoid confusion, is five times Tasmanian super bantamweight martial arts champion.

Tonight he will be fighting in the featherweight division at rock venue, Palais, in St Kilda.

Both have been training extremely hard for the competition, two daily sessions, six days a week, for two months.

If Tri and "Bear" win, they will be selected in the Australian team to compete in the world kickboxing titles in Perth in January.

● Tri Tri Tran gives reporter James Bresnehan a torrid time while training at the Glenorchy YMCA yesterday.

Tri Tri Tran and Florian Sonner, Hobart, 1986.

The Vietnamese Australians: Heritage and Contributions by Minh Hiền

Việt Võ training has positive influences on my second elder-brother, Trí Tuệ, long after he stopped practising it. Tuệ was a senior Việt Võ instructor and manager for most of Việt Võ fighters in both State and National Championships in the 1980s and 1990s.

Tuệ has always applied what he learnt from Việt Võ to control his mind and body as well as moral values such as respect for others, faithfulness and patience, influencing his decisions.

'Golf is the Game Of Love and Friendships,' said Tuệ.

In 2009, Tuệ and eleven friends founded the *Australian Vietnamese Golf Association* (AVGA). Since then, Tuệ has played golf a few times a week.

He has travelled all over Australia and Việt Nam for his GOLF, singing '*Home Is Where the Heart Is*' by Elvis Presley.

Trí Tuệ has travelled wide and far with his companion since 2009.

One of Tuệ's favourite golf courses is the *Barnbougle Dunes, Tasmania*.

"Fore!"

*Gió bỗng đâu về banh rẽ lối
Trôi dạt nơi nao nhớ muôn vàn...*

*Suddenly wind returns, the ball flies a new path,
Drifting somewhere and leaving me with countless memories ...*

Trí Tuệ's poem, translated by Minh Hiền.

Trí Tuệ, Barnbougle Dunes, Tasmania, 2022.

Another of Tuệ's favourite golf course is the *Cape Wickham Golf Links, Tasmania*.

Biển xanh bao bọc Wickham
Sân golf tuyệt mỹ ngất ngây tâm hồn
Fairways uốn lượn ngặt nghèo
Lại thêm lắm dốc thêm đèo cản ngăn
Bãi lùa hiểm hóc lại nhanh
Gió đâu bỗng lại lừa anh nữa rồi.

Blue Ocean surrounds Wickham
This beautiful golf course fascinates my soul
Fairways are tightly curved
With many slope and passes
And dangerous spots, I act fast
Then the wind suddenly deceives me again.

Trí Tuệ's poem, translated by Minh Hiền.

Trí Tuệ, Cape Wickham Golf Links, Tasmania, 2022.

Resilience

Resilience is one of the benefits of learning Martial Arts.

Members of Tri's Việt Võ faced many challenges and obstacles in their training.

Some days, a student might feel like they had the strength to take on the world. Other days, they felt down. No matter how they felt, when they turned up to Tri's training sessions, Tri and other senior members of the team did what they could to help the students get the most out of their training.

With practice, they built their resilience.

When a student said to Tri, 'I had a bad training session today, or I'm terrible today.'

Tri advised, 'All training sessions are good. Never bad. Not training is bad. *Savouring it, because, you can't swim in the same river twice.*'

To be able to win two different National Championships within a four-month period in 1984, Tri had practiced thousands and thousands of repetition of techniques over many years.

He did not just practice difficult techniques of kicking and punching but also running, skipping and, *dynamic tension* training.

Tri Minh Tran (Bé) and Tri Tri Tran, Training in a park, Hobart, 1982.

The Vietnamese Australians: Heritage and Contributions by Minh Hiền

Bé and Tri running in a park, Hobart, 1982.

Tri, the University of Tasmania, Sandy Bay, 1980.

Tri, the University of Tasmania, Sandy Bay, 1981.

According to Tuệ, golf can best be defined as an endless series of tragedies obscured by an occasional miracle.

Môn golf đáng ghét quá bạn ơi
Cần có par lại gấp đôi rồi
Điểm hay nhất nay mười năm lẻ
Bao giờ chơi được "bảy hai" thôi!

Golf is a game, that men love to hate,
You needed a four, but you just got an eight,
Your best score has stood now, for ten years or more,
It's unlikely you'll ever beat that "seventy two".

Trí Tuệ's poem, translated by Minh Hiền.

Trí Tuệ, St Michael's Golf Course, Sydney, November 2019.

*Đời người dâu bể nắng mưa
Dẫu rằng bạc tóc vẫn chưa hiểu đời
Chơi golf cũng vậy bạn ơi
Nay hay mai dở cuộc đời khác chi.*

*Life is filled with sunshine and rain
Even though my hair is grey, I still don't understand
Playing golf is the same, my friend
Today's good, tomorrow's bad, life is no different.*

Trí Tuệ's poem, translated by Minh Hiền.

Trí Tuệ at Hoiana Shores Golf Course, Hội An, Việt Nam.

Golf is an outdoor activity, so Tuệ needs to be resilient, especially during the Covid-19 lockdown. On 11 October 2021, Tuệ celebrated Sydney coming out of lockdown after 100 days.

> *Hello Life!*
> *"If Loving You is Wrong*
> *... I don't want to be right"*

Sydney coming out of 100 days of lockdown on 31 October 2021, the news headlines:

> *88% fully vaccinated,*
> *94% first dose...*
> *Travelling can restart...*
>
> *Lâu lắm rồi mới ra sân trở lại*
> *Bao tháng ngày trong thế giới lockdown*
> *Là xa cách bây giờ ta nếm đủ*
> *Khi ôm cây lúc ủ rũ trong đầm*
>
> *It has been a while since I have been on the field again*
> *Days and months in the world of lockdown*
> *Isolation we now have had enough*
> *Hugging a tree, I can feel its sadness.*

Trí Tuệ's poem, translated by Minh Hiền.

Trí Tuệ, Sydney coming out of 100 days of lockdown, 31 October 2021.

The massive rain, a largest amount of water pouring out from the sky over a thirty-year period, does not stop Tuệ from his golf.

Sân golf vắng ngắt dăm người lại
Thảm cỏ mênh mang đọng nước đầy
Sân vắng golfers ngồi ngán ngẩm
Kìa gió heo may kéo đến gần ...

Tầm tả mưa rơi muôn hạt ngọc
Bãi lùa ngập nước ngỡ dòng sông
Lùa banh, banh lướt trên làn sóng
Hố mãi nằm chờ bóng đến không

The golf course is deserted, just a few people
The vast grass carpet is full of water
The course is empty, golfers are bored
Behold, the wind draws near...

The rain is pouring down thousands of pearls
The flooded field looks like a river
Slide the ball, it surfs on the wave
The hole is forever waiting for the ball to come

Trí Tuệ's poem, translated by Minh Hiền.

Trí Tuệ, Golfing in the rain, Sydney, 2021.

Resilience paid off, on 4 February 2023, the first week that Tuệ played golf in *the New Year of the Precious Cat, Tết Qúi Mão*, he won the *Gold Medallist Winner of the Year at the Cromer Golf Course*. He won by one stroke with the score of -2 on a stroke play event from black tee. Tuệ said, 'Even though, this is a Cromer Golf Club honour board annual event, it seems only a resident local long neck turtle on hole 10th came out to watch and a few birds singing some encouraging songs along the fairways, it was nevertheless a great day for golf with clear sky, breezes, 26 degrees Celsius, 9.9 green speed, firm fairways … The golf season has only just started. Hope to see everyone at the Tết Championship next Wednesday at the Coast Golf Club and in Melbourne in March for the VVGA Open Championship followed by the Sydney monthly medals at Mona Vale Golf Club a week after…'

Trí Tuệ, Sydney, 4 February 2023.

Phong cảnh nơi đây tựa trong tranh
Thảm cỏ xanh xanh bước chẳng đành
Sương tan dưới ánh bình minh nắng
Cờ cắm sau đồi thử thách anh...

Here, the scenery is like a painting
Lush green grass I am reluctant to step on
The mist melts under the rays of dawn
The flag is placed behind the hill to challenge me...

Trí Tuệ's poem, translated by Minh Hiền.

For the record: Tuệ shot the first under par (nett) in six months!

Cromer Golf Course, Sydney, August 2022.
Photo courtesy of Tri Tue Tran.

Tournaments

Both Tri and Tuệ organised many Martial Arts tournaments and State Open Championships during the 1980s and the 1990s which demanded a great deal of their time.

Tri Tri Tran, Quarter Final, Australian Open, Melbourne, 1986.

To prepare for Championship tournaments, Tri and his students trained every day.

Tri and his student at the University of Tasmania's gym.

When Tri prepared Bé for the *South Pacific Championship*, every morning before going to work Tri and Bé ran ten kilometres together and they did some stretching exercises before and after. Then after work, they punched and kicked sandbags for an hour, then practised movements for another hour.

The Vietnamese Australians: Heritage and Contributions by Minh Hiền

Tri wrote the following article:

Improving Your Physical Condition for Contact Tournament

Many people are aware that it would be good for them to be "in good shape".

But do they really know what bring in good physical condition means? Do you?

If you go along to a Martial Arts Club and train twice a week, you are getting exercise and learning a little of the skill, but whether or not you can attain total physical fitness for contact tournament depends not only on how regularly you train, but how strenuously you train and what extra physical activity besides training once or twice a week at your club.

All Martial Arts instructors, no matter what style of Martial Arts they're teaching, will agree with me that one can improve his technique by becoming more physically fit and flexible. And, for contact tournament, physical fitness is the most important factor for winning.

Running

Long distance running is beneficial for contact tournament fighters, but doesn't necessarily give the require help. Sprinting short distances – fifty to a hundred metres – seems to be more appropriate for fighters than long distance running.

Several weeks before my competition, I always do ten series of sprints (eight metres each) four times a week. Remember, before you sprint all out, always do warm up exercises thoroughly, especially the ham string and calf muscles.

Perhaps a slow jog for ½ a mile following the warm-up exercises and before the sprint would be best.

And always do stretching exercises (warm-down) after the sprint, if you want your leg muscles to tighten up – this resulting in lack of flexibility for high and fact kicking.

Skipping

Skipping is beneficial to the cardiovascular and respiratory systems of the body, just as running is. Also, skipping can greatly improve your foot-work (if done properly).

While practising Martial Arts, most of us train bare-footed, you should not skip bare-footed. Although I know that skipping is a necessary routine for my conditioning program, it can become quite boring. To overcome this, I try to skip while listening to my favourite music.

Dynamic Tension

Dynamic Tension is muscle contraction with movement and without weights. If you have seen a second-degree black-belt fellow (or higher) performing a pattern (kata), you will probably notice some techniques are performed in sequence, at an extremely slow speed but with maximum contraction of the muscle groups involved in the performance of that specific technique. The advantages of this particular strength training exercise (*Dynamic Tension*) are:
1- You can correct your technique at the same time as building up your strength.
2- Improving respiratory and cardiovascular fitness as well as physical strength.
3- Your muscles will increase very little in size (if you consider that an advantage)

4- It is a perfect exercise if you want to improve your fitness and strength but have some injuries (e.g. ankle sprains).
5- Maintaining proper muscle tone without affecting your flexibility.

I don't really understand why *dynamic tension* should only be taught at advanced level (black-belt onward). To me, everyone who has been doing Martial Arts for longer than six months should be taught *dynamic tension*. My students are taught *dynamic tension* as soon as they master the few basic techniques such as: straight-punch; reverse-push; upper-block; front kick etc. ... One important point you should bear in mind, whilst practising *dynamic tension* you should never hold your breath.

Tri and his students trained regularly to prepare for their tournaments.

Tri and his students training for the tournament at the University of Tasmania gym.

Paul Hunt, four times *Tasmanian Open Champion* and twice *Australian Open Kung Fu Champion* with Georgia Mars at Việt Võ Hobart club. Georgia, later, did obtain her black-belt in Việt Võ as she always wanted. She's currently an Art teacher in Tasmania.

The Vietnamese Australians: Heritage and Contributions by Minh Hiền

A VIETNAMESE FIGHTING SYSTEM

TRAINING HALL: SANDOWN HOCKEY CLUB
SANDY BAY

TRAINING: WEDNESDAY & FRIDAY
6.00 to 8.00 PM

WEEKEND TRAINING: SATURDAY 2.00 to 4.00 PM
AT: UNIVERSITY OF TASMANIA
SPORTS CENTRE SANDY BAY

'Exposure to difficult techniques at the early stages of learning also allows students to more easily incorporate them into their development as they progress'

A. Knife hand block defends against left jab.

B. Shift to the right & deliver left roundhouse kick.

C. right elbow to the upper back.

Tri at the University of Tasmania gym, Sandy Bay.

Tri's student, Robert, testing the strength of the tiles before using them in a real demonstration, Hobart.

Tri Minh Tran (Bé) testing the strength of the tiles before using them in a real demonstration, Hobart.

Tri Minh Tran (Bé), the University of Tasmania, Sandy Bay.

Tri Minh Tran (Bé), Sandy Bay, 1983.

Tasmanian trio claims national kung fu titles

FRI 9/9/88

TASMANIAN kung fu exponents fared well at the Australian titles in Melbourne last weekend.

Tri Tri Tran took four of his Viet Vo Dao fighters to the national kung fu championship, and three returned with titles.

Tran won the Australian under 60kg title for the sixth consecutive year.

He fought three bouts, each ended by knockout within the first 30 seconds of the opening round.

For the title he beat Canadian national kung fu champion Warren Stratulate, who had studied Tran's style of fighting over the past year in readiness for the bout.

Unfortunately for Stratulate, Tran injured his right knee during his second bout, so changed his attack to the left leg and caught the Canadian off guard.

Paul Hunt, a former Tasmanian middleweight karate champion and part-time amateur boxer, won the Australian under 64kg title.

He had five fights, and won the final by knockout, beating Robert Balance.

Louisa Harpham became the first Australian women's lightweight champion — it was the first time a national women's kung fu championship was held.

The other team member, Clinton Wastell, was eliminated in the first round.

Tasmania's three national kung fu champions, from left, Paul Hunt, Louisa Harpham and Tri Tri Tran.

Tri took his students to the 1988 National Kung Fu Championship in Melbourne and they won three National Kung Fu titles, 9 September 1988.

Tri Tri Tran, Australian Open Kung Fu Championship, Melbourne Town Hall, 1984.

The Vietnamese Australians: Heritage and Contributions by Minh Hiền

Tri Tri Tran and his student, Florian Sonner, Sydney, September 1984.

Florian was the youngest ever Australian Open Champion at the age of seventeen. He needed the written approval of both of his parents and his Việt Võ teacher to be allowed to compete.

Preceding the tournaments or by invitation, my three brothers and Tri's students also demonstrated Việt Võ to the publics.

Tuệ and Tri's student demonstrated at a community hall in Hobart.

Tri demonstrated at the Rooke Mall in Devonport, North of Tasmania.

Standing in the photo is Mick Meer, who was Tri's student, Việt Võ senior instructor and head instructor of Devonport Việt Võ club at the time. Later Mick became a Việt Võ teacher and a Senior Army Officer in the Australian Reserve Army. Mick was also a senior banker. After Mick left Devonport, Mick Spillers became the head instructor.

Tri's student, Paul Hunt, demonstrated at the University of Tasmania.

Tri and Tuệ also trained many children for tournaments.

Kate arms herself and is ready to meet the challenge of attack

Kate Spencer, one of the first junior black-belts at the time and the darling baby of the Việt Võ Hobart club. Kate has become a lawyer, practising in Sydney since around 2000.

The Vietnamese Australians: Heritage and Contributions by Minh Hiền

Peter Scanlon and Jake Mars training at the University of Tasmania.

Ten years after this photo, Jake did achieve his MA dream by obtaining his black-belt. Jake latter became a teacher and taught overseas for many years.

Peter Scanlon had just achieved a junior Việt Võ black-belt when he had to move to QLD with his parents. There was no Việt Võ school in QLD for him to continue his training as Peter and his father had wished. Tri and Tuệ advised and wrote a letter of recommendation for Peter to a leading Taekwondo club. Peter joined Taekwondo and a few years later became Australian Taekwondo Champion and an Olympian who represented Australia Taekwondo at the 1988 Summer Olympics.

After Tri left Tasmania to work overseas, Bé became the Head Teacher of Việt Võ in Hobart. When Bé left Hobart to work in Canberra, he and another black-belt holder also from the Hobart club, started a Việt Võ club in Canberra, while Steve Mars took over as the Head teacher in Hobart. After Steve left, Graham Lush and Andrew Fulton were Head Teachers. Graham had just finished his PhD at that time and Andrew had finished his Commerce degree and worked for the government.

In Sydney, after teaching Việt Võ at the Dong Tam association's hall in Fairfield for more than ten years, Tri left to work overseas. Việt Võ Sydney has produced many good Việt Võ teachers and instructors such as Thai Nguyen, Cuong Le, Ha Lam and Nick.

Nowadays, even though Tri is still training most days, he has withdrawn from regular teaching activities. He teaches only a few senior black-belt trainees once a week.

Charcoal sketch by Tri's daughter (Ellyse Tran - aged 16) in 2023.

For the past fifteen years, Trí Tuệ has organised many Golf tournaments both in Australia and in Việt Nam. He is one of the founders of the Australian Vietnamese Golf Association, AVGA, and has been the AVGA Captain since its establishment in 2009.

The AVGA head quarter is in Sydney with over 200 members. Each state in Australia has its own association and they organise their own local social and competitions.

Golf encourages quality time and bonding, plus physical and emotional benefits. AVGA's competitions and activities provide opportunities for all family members to participate.

Together with his friends at the AVGA, Trí Tuệ organised golf tournaments and the annual AVGA Open Championships to promote Vietnamese culture in Australia and Overseas and, to create opportunities for business networking and raise funds for charities through golf.

It has become a tradition that the most important event of the year among Vietnamese golfers in Australia is the annual AVGA Open Championships which are held on the first Sunday in November each year.

The AVGA annual championship has grown from the modest budget of less than $1000 (for trophies) in 2009 to well over $100,000 ten years later and at the 2019 championship it included some fabulous holiday trips to Việt Nam, quality designer championship shirts and caps, beautiful trophies, golfing equipment and substantial amounts of cash on offer for a Hole in One on all of the par 3s.

Trí Tuệ opening the 10th AVGA Open Championships, Sydney, November 2019.

Trí Tuệ with golfers at the 10th AVGA Open Championships, Sydney, November 2019.

Minh Hiền and Trí Tuệ at the AVGA dinner, Sydney, November 2019.

Tuệ has also been the President of the Overseas Vietnamese Golf Association, OVGA, since its establishment in 2015. The OVGA has members worldwide in more than eighteen countries and is growing.

Trí Tuệ at the OVGA Open Championships, Hạ Long, 2019.

Hạ Long cảnh đẹp nhiều thử thách
Thổn thức chờ mong bóng tối tàn
Bình minh phát bóng sương se lạnh
Bồng lai tiên cảnh ắt còn ganh

Hạ Long's beautiful scenery brings many challenges
Anxiously waiting for the darkness to end
Dawn shines with chilly dew
Bồng lai fairyland must still be jealous.

Trí Tuệ's poem, translated by Minh Hiền.

Trí Tuệ at the OVGA, Ha Long Golf Course, Hạ Long, 2019.

Trí Tuệ at the OVGA Open Championships, Hội An, Việt Nam, 2023.

My Writing Journey

My father was born in a village in the North.

In 1954, when Việt Nam was divided at the Bến Hải River, he was a married man with a baby son. He left the North, thinking that he would go to the South first then he would return to take his parents, wife and son to the South with him.

My father boarded at my mother's mother's house on the Southern bank of the Bến Hải River for one year.

Three years later, he married my mother. The war lasted twenty-one years so he never saw his parents again. The memories haunted him for many decades.

My father was a teacher and my mother was an *áo dài* maker in Quảng Ngãi, a small town in central Việt Nam, where Tri, Tuệ and I were born.

My father at the river where he first met my mother, Quảng Trị, Việt Nam, 2007.

Traditionally, many Vietnamese believe that people's careers can be foretold on their first birthdays. On that day the child's parents put many items on the floor, such as a pen, a comb, a pair of scissors, a doll, colourful picture books, a textbook, a measurement tape, a piece of cloth, a mirror, etc. The one-year-old child is then encouraged to pick up an item, and the first item that the child picks up indicates the child's future desirable career.

My mother told me, 'On your first birthday, you first picked up your father's book and then his pen.'

In 1964, when I was a one-year old, the government of the South Việt Nam appointed my father to a position of the principal in the newly created high school in Đức Phổ.

Minh Hiền with her mother and brother Trí Tuệ, Nha Trang, Việt Nam, 1964.

This new school was in the Strategic Hamlet region, part of a program implemented on the advice of a British adviser by the government of the South. It had begun in 1960. Đức Phổ was heavily infiltrated by the North Vietnamese Communist, Việt Cộng, and one of the most dangerous places in South Việt Nam. The purpose of the Strategic Hamlets was to separate the Việt Cộng, from civilians.

The Vietnamese Australians: Heritage and Contributions by Minh Hiền

My father could not refuse the government's decision so he took my mother, my brothers and me to Húê while he was working as the high school principal in Đức Phổ. While we were living in Huế, my father went back and forth between Huế, Quảng Ngãi and Đức Phổ. From Quảng Ngãi to the high school in Đức Phổ, he was transported by military helicopter, with a soldier on each side who carried heavy machine guns, ready to shoot any suspicious Việt Cộng under their flight path. My mother was constantly in fear, worrying that the Việt Cộng would kidnap my father and drag him into the jungle or cut his throat. So every week, my mother took us to the *Thiên Mụ* Temple to pray.

One year later, my father was appointed to a position in Sài Gòn and he moved all of us there. Bé was born in Sài Gòn the following year.

Minh Hiền with her brothers, Sài Gòn, Việt Nam, 1969.

When my brothers and I were children, we often studied together at a large table. I took my studies very seriously.

Growing up in Việt Nam during the 1970s, I was educated at school as well as at home.

At school, I loved studying mathematics, literature and history. By way of education at home, my mother taught me *Công, Dung, Ngôn, Hạnh*.

My mother worked from home as a dressmaker. While making clothes, she often sang. Sometimes she sang folk songs, sometimes verses from the Vietnamese Classics, and sometimes verses from the Opera Show. I loved to hear my mother's voice. When she told a story, the tone of her voice changed as she narrated the scenes in the stories and I always felt as if she were singing the play. She had a beautiful voice. Her accent was a mixture of Quảng Trị and the Royal City Huế; when she recounted stories, read poetry or sang, her tones were peaceful, yet they often brought tears of nostalgia and a yearning for peace to her listeners.

Whilst my mother was working, I played in the front yard and sometimes I sat beside her. One day my father brought me a table, a chair, a pencil and some coloured papers and my mother brought me scissors and made a little space for me within her sight. Then every day as I watched her cutting material to make clothes, I cut paper dresses. I would pick up my scissors with my left hand and a piece of paper in my right hand and cut them into all sort of shapes and sizes. This was the beginning of my in-house learning; at home my parents never forced us to conform to any strict order but at school I would be forced to write with my right hand. To this day I cannot hold a pen properly, but I can cut very well. When I was in my teens, my mother taught me dressmaking, cooking and took me to opera shows.

I have wanted to write about lives of ordinary Vietnamese and of history since I was a child. When I came to Australia, I knew very little English and I was very good at Mathematics. Hence, I studied for an Engineering degree.

I had always wanted to improve my English, but studying for an engineering degree had demanded all of my time. During my undergraduate course, I learnt the English technical words that helped me to understand engineering subjects.

After my graduation and when I was in the first year of my Master's degree, I enrolled in an evening English class. This was where I met Farshid.

Throughout my adult life I had applied my capabilities with numbers to earn a living. I worked hard by nature. And so with a busy working life, I rarely read non-technical books.

One day, in 2003, I read a travel article in a magazine. The article was about Vietnamese noodle soup, phở, but the author described it in such a manner that it captured my attention and transported me to my motherland, made me hungry and nostalgic.

By that time, Việt Nam began to welcome the whole world with open arms. People from Australia, Cambodia, China, France, Japan and the US were traveling freely throughout Việt Nam. The US President George Bush was welcomed by children waving flags all the way from the airport to his hotel. George Bush and John Howard, Prime Minister of Australia, could go for a walk and eat at a local restaurant, just as we did.

Farshid commented that he could not imagine that it would ever happen in his country of birth, Iran.

'Perhaps it is possible for the Vietnamese to forgive because most Vietnamese are Buddhists,' Farshid said.

'Perhaps it is in the Vietnamese blood. It is in our DNA,' I said. 'We do not hesitate to fight for our rights but deep down in our hearts we want peace.'

I had learnt that for thousands of years the Vietnamese had fought fearlessly against powerful invaders and then they worked with the former enemies once the war was over.

It had been thirty years after the Fall of Saigon. The Vietnamese had put the war behind them and, I had returned to Việt Nam many times.

I decided to learn to become a writer. It took me three years to study for a Master of Creative Writing and to write my first book, *My Heritage: Vietnam fatherland motherland.*

The writing of *My Heritage* helped me to reflect on our lives in Việt Nam.

Thảnh thơi dưới ánh chiều tà
Ung dung đọc sách nhớ ngày tháng qua
Ao kia cũng có cội nguồn
Đời người ai chẳng khi buồn lúc vui
Đây là một mảnh đời tôi
Tương lai trước mặt cội nguồn mãi thương.

Relaxing under the western sun,
Leisurely reading 'My Heritage',
Feeling nostalgic about the old days,
Even the lake has its heritage,
Life has joys and of course sorrows,
Here's a piece of my life,
A bright future always springs up from the lovely roots.

Trí Tuệ's poem, translated by Minh Hiền.

Minh Hiền one year after her last chemotherapy session, January 2020.

The reading of *My Heritage* helped me to overcome adversities. Since recovering from breast cancer, I have wanted to write about *Vietnamese Australians*.

We launched the first book of the *Vietnamese Australians* series on 23 April 2023 to celebrate the *World Book and Copyright Day and the English Language Day*. It contains a collection of poems and short stories written by me about Vietnamese traditions and about myself who risked life in a small fishing boat to pursue education and thirty-eight years later while undergoing treatment for breast cancer successfully stood up for my rights against a giant public employer. It recounts the cultural activities, events, people and places that have featured in my life, illustrated with colourful photographs and paintings. It shows the influence of Vietnamese culture, historical and mythological figures, language and poetry on my actions and decisions.

This book is the second book of the series. It has taken me five years to convince my brothers to let me write a book about their contributions to Australian society through sport. Like most Vietnamese men and women it is hard for them to think that someone would want to read their life stories. In my view everyone has a story to write and someone will benefit from reading it. Growing up with my three brothers, both in Việt Nam and in Australia, I have always admired them: their courage, their passions for sport, their humanity, their gentleness, their practising of the five virtues: *Nhân, Lễ, Nghĩa, Trí, Tín* - Benevolence, Propriety, Righteousness, Wisdom and Trustworthiness.

My eldest brother Trí Tri literarily gave all his youth and beyond to Australians through his unique skills in Vietnamese Martial Arts. Tri has introduced thousands of people from all walks of life to the philosophy and the spirit of Việt Võ. Till this day many of his students regard him and his teaching methods very highly. Many call him the *Việt Võ legend, Tri Tri Tran*.

My second-elder brother Trí Tuệ spent great energy organising events and connecting people. While living in Hobart, Tuệ arranged and participated in hundreds of State and National Martial Arts Championships. For these matches Tuệ also managed the Tasmanian Việt Võ team offering endless support. In Sydney, Tuệ turned to golf and organised and participated in hundreds of golf tournaments and dinners in Australia and in Việt Nam, paved the way for many Australians to experience another aspect of multicultural degustation.

The Vietnamese Australians: Heritage and Contributions by Minh Hiền　　　　　　　　p.109

My younger brother Minh Trí spent all his youth practising Vietnamese Martial Arts while studying at high school, then university. He came to Australia as a refugee aged fifteen and became a role model for many young people in Hobart. He demonstrated that it was possible to complete a degree in IT at university while practising martial arts and winning six *State Championships* and the *Australian and South Pacific Championship*. Minh Trí also held the fort and led the Việt Võ team in Hobart for many years while Tri was working overseas. Later he introduced the philosophy and the spirit of Việt Võ to young people in Canberra during the late 1990s.

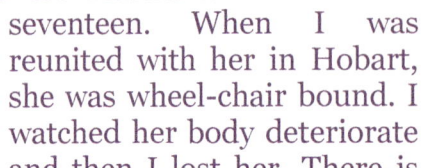

For me, I left my mother for Australia when I was seventeen. When I was reunited with her in Hobart, she was wheel-chair bound. I watched her body deteriorate and then I lost her. There is no cure for motor neurone disease (MND). My mother passed away at the age of fifty but her spirit has never left me. My mother was forced to leave school when she lost her father at the age of eight; a casualty of colonialism. She was never able to go back to school. She started sewing and became a talented dressmaker. She made beautiful áo dài, the traditional costume for Vietnamese women. Before MND robbed her of her strength, she taught hundreds of girls and women the art of dressmaking and supported them until they could make their own living. Her life has inspired me. In the various jobs I have had in Australia I was always looking for ways to assist others to improve their capabilities. I prepared manuals, in my own time, to assist thousands of employees in understanding and improving their financial and accounting skills. I have a great passion for learning and teaching. In addition to my work here in Australia I have developed lessons for young Vietnamese whom I teach on line, opening their minds, raising their ambitions and creating opportunities they would not otherwise have.

My mother was not able to witness the many things that my brothers and I have achieved in our lives.

We have succeeded because of her love and motherly care.

I hope that by writing this book I have shown my gratitude and that my mother's spirit is happy.

Minh Hiền with her brothers Sydney, April 2021.

The Vietnamese Australians: Heritage and Contributions by Minh Hiền

The third book of the series will be about *Culture, History, Entertainment and Food*. Some parts of the book will cover the Vietnamese contribution to Australian society through entertainment and food.

Minh Hiền with her parents, siblings, adopted sister, uncles and cousin, Sài Gòn, 1975.

Minh Hiền, Super Full Moon, 7 May 2020, Drummoyne, Sydney.

*Minh Hiền and Farshid's extended dining room,
Saigonese Food and Arts, Murray Street, Hobart, 1995.*

Minh Hiền at home, raising hens for eggs for Saigonese Food and Arts, Hobart, 1995.

The Vietnamese Australians: Heritage and Contributions by Minh Hiền

Minh Hiền and Farshid's extended front garden, Sydney, January 2020.

Minh Hiền on the way to the HardCopy seminar with Farshid, September 2019.

References

1. https://www.homeaffairs.gov.au/mca/files/2016-cis-vietnam.PDF
2. https://holylandvietnamstudies.com/blog/an-attempt-to-study-the-cultural-history-of-traditional-vietnamese-martial-arts-section-1/
3. https://en.wikipedia.org/wiki/Trần_Hưng_Đạo (downloaded 5 October 2023)
4. https://www.britannica.com/biography/Tran-Hung-Dao (downloaded 5 Oct 2023)
5. https://en.wikipedia.org/wiki/Quang_Trung (downloaded 5 October 2023)
6. https://vov2.vov.vn/van-hoa-giai-tri/nu-tuong-bui-thi-xuan-22308.vov2
7. Mark Cutts (ed.), The State of the World's Refugees 2000: Fifty years of humanitarian action, UNHCR 2000.
8. Tasmanian Museum and Art Gallery (TMAG) Annual Report 2008–09 (p. 37) www.tmag.tas.gov.au/__data/assets/pdf_file/0008/66671/TMAG_Annual_Report_2008-09.pdf (downloaded 15 October 2023)

Acknowledgements

My warmest thanks go to my three brothers, *Trí Tri, Trí Tuệ and Minh Trí*, for sharing their stories and photos with me.

I thank my niece, *Ellyse Tran*, for the paintings which she did for me that are included in this book.

I thank my English teacher, *Margaret Eldridge AM*, for proofreading and writing a foreword for this book.

I thank my brother *Trí Tri* for allowing me to include the photos of his daughter *Ellyse Tran*'s paintings and the photos that were taken by him or for him.

I thank my brothers *Trí Tuệ* and *Minh Trí* for allowing me to use the photos that were taken by them or for them.

I thank various people (as noted in the captions of some photos) for allowing me to use the photos that they took.

I wish to acknowledge my husband, *Farshid Anvari*, for photographing most of my photos and for restoring old photos.

Every effort has been made to trace copyright holders of the photographic material included in this book. I would appreciate hearing from any copyright holders not here acknowledged.

Above all are my memories of my mother; her spirit has given me strength to overcome the many difficulties I have faced in my life. Her life has inspired me to write this book.

Milton Keynes UK
Ingram Content Group UK Ltd.
UKHW050322021223
433634UK00003B/81